Praise for *Breath for the Bones*

"*Breath for the Bones* is a marvelous repository of Luci Shaw's accumulated wisdom about literature and imagination as they intersect with the Christian faith. This book has something for everyone. For readers who are just beginning their acquaintance with Luci's ideas about the artistic imagination, this book is a veritable gift package with everything included. For me, as someone who has assimilated Luci's thinking about the arts for four decades, reading the book was like attending a party—meeting familiar friends (favorite quotations and vintage Luci Shaw statements) and being introduced to new acquaintances (material put before me for the first time)."

Leland Ryken [Clyde S. Kilby]
Professor of English, Wheaton College

"Gentle and probing, rich in wisdom, and reflecting years of experience as a remarkable poet of faith, Luci Shaw's *Breath for the Bones* is worth pondering deeply. I commend it most warmly."

Jeremy Begbie
Associate Director, Institute of Theology,
Imagination and the Arts, University of St Andrews

"Like the amphibians she admires, Luci Shaw breathes vitality from visible and invisible spheres, and invites us to do the same. Reading this book refreshes faith and kindles artistic expression."

Susan S. Phillips, Ph.D.
Executive Director, New College Berkeley, Graduate Theological Union
Lecturer, Fuller Theological Seminary,
Regent College, and San Francisco Theological Seminary
Editor of *The Crisis of Care*

"Sometimes you look at a piece of writing and say, 'yes, that's it.' Something fundamental about craft in the light of faith has struck its cord."

Diane Glancy
Professor, Macalester College
Author of *Asylum in the Grasslands, Rooms New
and Selected Poems, The Dance Partner*, and *In-Between Places*

"'Beauty matters,' Luci Shaw says in this wide-ranging and lovely new book. Grounded in her lifelong commitment to art and faith, *Breath for the Bones* is part contemplation, and part practical companion for artists of faith—giving readers wise and sustaining guidance for what may be the deepest journey they ever make."

Erin McGraw
Author of *The Good Life*

"Luci Shaw has been a faithful bugler, so to speak, calling us all to wake up to—to what? To the Creation, forsooth. To the Incarnation. To the Sacraments. To Poetry. Four things Luci is all about. Listen to her."

Thomas Howard
Author of *Dove Descending: An Inquiry into T. S. Eliot's "Four Quartets"* and *On Being Catholic*

"This book offers a fascinating glimpse into the writing life of one of our most beloved poets. In a deeply personal exploration of what it means to write, Luci Shaw narrates episodes from experience, quotes her own journal, gives sane and generous counsel, and cites the wisdom of her mentors. The exercises and questions at the end of each chapter provide splendid, practical ways to help readers begin writing."

Jeanne Murray Walker
Professor of English, University of Delaware

"With an attentive heart toward the work of her Creator, Luci Shaw weaves together a celebration of words and images. Anchored in faith and mystery, *Breath for the Bones* inspires listening with inner ears and opening the eyes of the heart to embrace our own creative gifts, pointing us toward the Eternal."

Rev. Paul-Gordon Chandler
Rector, St. John's Episcopal Church
Cairo, Egypt

"Luci Shaw's *Breath for the Bones* provides profound insight into the most important questions about what it means to be human, to have imagination, to be creative, and to be image-bearers of a creative God. And it does so in a way that befits a poet: the work is as beautiful as it is thoughtful—it incarnates the same artistry that Luci so articulately invites her readers to seek after."

Matthew Dickerson
Author of *Ents, Elves, and Eriador: The Environmental Vision of J. R. R. Tolkien* and *From Homer to Harry Potter: A Handbook on Myth and Fantasy*
Director of the New England Young Writers Conference
Professor at Middlebury College, VT

Breath *for* *the* Bones

ART, IMAGINATION, AND SPIRIT

by Luci Shaw

THOMAS NELSON
Since 1798

NASHVILLE   DALLAS   MEXICO CITY   RIO DE JANEIRO   BEIJING

Published in Nashville, TN, by Thomas Nelson. Thomas Nelson is a trademark of Thomas Nelson, Inc.

Thomas Nelson titles may be purchased in bulk for educational, business, fund-raising, or sales promotional use. For information, please e-mail SpecialMarkets@ThomasNelson.com.

Published in association with the literary agency of Alive Communications, Inc., 7680 Goddard Street, Suite 200, Colorado Springs, Colorado 80920, www.alivecommunications.com.

Scripture references are from the following sources:

The HOLY BIBLE: NEW INTERNATIONAL VERSION® (NIV). Copyright © 1973, 1978, 1984, International Bible Society. Used by permission of Zondervan Publishing House.

The King James Version of the Bible (KJV).

The Message (MSG) by Eugene H. Peterson. Copyright © 1993, 1994, 1995, 1996, 2000. Used by permission of NavPress Publishing Group.

THE NEW KING JAMES VERSION (NKJV), copyright © 1979, 1980, 1982, Thomas Nelson, Inc., Publishers.

The NEW REVISED STANDARD VERSION of the Bible (NRSV). Copyright © 1989 by the Division of Christian Education of the National Council of the Churches of Christ in the U.S.A.

The Good News Bible

The NEW AMERICAN STANDARD BIBLE, © Copyright The Lockman Foundation 1960, 1962, 1963, 1968, 1971, 1972, 1973, 1975, 1995. Used by permission.

The *Holy Bible*, New Living Translation, copyright © 1996. used by permission of Tyndale House Publishers, Inc., Wheaton, Illinois 60189. All rights reserved.

The REVISED STANDARD VERSION of the Bible. Copyright © 1946, 1952, 1971, 1973, by the Division Christian education of the National Council of the Churches of Christ in the U.S.A. Used by permission.

The Holy Bible, English Standard Version. Copyright © 2001 by Crossway Bibles, a division of Good News Publishers.

Library of Congress Cataloging-in-Publication Data

Shaw, Luci.
    Breath for the bones : art, imagination, and spirit / by Luci Shaw.
      p. cm.
    ISBN 978-0-8499-0334-2 (hardcover)
    1. Artists—Religious life. 2. Creation (Literary, artistic, etc.)—Religious aspects—Christianity. 3. Christianity and the arts. I. Title.
    BV4596.A78S53 2007
    261.5'7—dc22

        2006100153

Printed in the United States of America

07 08 09 10 11 12 QW 9 8 7 6 5 4 3 2 1

contents

note to readers

This book is the compilation of many poignant words found in Luci Shaw's writings, lecture notes, workshops, journals, interviews, essays, and poems. Any gaps and spaces throughout the text reflect the quilting together of these materials to form a meaningful sequence of concepts with a thought-provoking readability.

Some of this material was written during her life with and in the period immediately following the death of her first husband, Harold, who died in 1986. His last days were recorded in Luci's book *God in the Dark: Through Grief and Beyond.*

introduction

Just as you do not know how the breath
comes to the bones in the mother's womb,
so you do not know the work of God,
who makes everything.

ECCLESIASTES 11:5 NRSV

This verse from the Old Testament book of Ecclesiastes powerfully brings together the idea of the mystery of imagination with the influence of the Spirit and the creatorhood of God. It speaks to the artistic process from a profoundly God-centered perspective.

Such words of wisdom gave this book its title and somehow bring the themes of this book into living reality for me. They leap headfirst into the question of God's creatorhood as well as our need to wrestle with this question. The two are inseparable; for the artist who is a Christian the question is inevitably grapple with a two-pronged. Such an artist does not deal simply with matters of art or of faith, but with both. The double question we must always ask is, "How does faith inform art?" and "How can art animate faith?"

Which comes first? It's the old problem of the chicken and the egg. I find a possible model for solution in the word *intersections*. I see imagination and spirit as the warp and weft of loomed material, an interlacing of lengthwise faith and crosswise art that forms a fabric of integrity and beauty.

But first, please visualize with me an alternative model that may help clarify how faith and art work together—are breath for the bones to each other.

I hold in my imagination like a well-remembered dream the picture of a large, rambling house—old, with multiple doors and windows at different levels, all opening onto a landscape of fields interrupted by trees, and beyond them rolling hills, and even farther away, the glistening horizon of the ocean. The main body of the building has evidently been added onto over the years (I notice all sorts of odd adjuncts) but the whole structure is bound together by its underlying stone foundation and the shell of walls, beams, and roof that enclose and unify it.

Inside the building lives a diverse community, an extended family of people variously occupied—cooking, cleaning, studying, conversing, teaching, giving advice, receiving advice, listening, rehearsing, resting, making love, dreaming, creating. They are young and old, male and female, single and married, widowed and divorced, inexperienced and mature, naive and wise. They are school children, parents, laborers, teachers, businesspeople, scholars, artists.

Moving among them, talking and working along with them, is an ordinary-looking man; it is the Christ, the One who lends the house its personal warmth, its structure, its creative center, its vision, its reason for being.

This is the house of faith. I have heard of it before. As I pass through the front door, I expect to see symbols of noble realities— shafts of light through stained-glass windows, a carved stone altar, kneelers, a gothic space vibrating with baroque organ music, per- haps a thoughtful sermon or philosophical discussion in progress. But as I look around at the mundane activity, I realize that faith is neither kindled into being, nor linked with life, only by such eccle- siastical paraphernalia, imagery, or atmosphere, nor by metaphysi- cal discourse and theology, but also by tone of voice, laughter or crying, eyes meeting, an atmosphere open to questions and ideas, hands meeting other hands, lifted in blessing or comfort, streaked with dirt from the garden, calloused from carpentry, sudsy from the dishpan, by windows wide open to sun and wind, the sounds of kids playing, and the smells of rain and manure and pine needles.

Wandering freely through the house, I particularly notice my kindred spirits, the artists: a sculptor with a blowtorch at work on a bronze abstract, a painter doing a preliminary charcoal sketch of a live model, a weaver adding to a length of tapestry with much clacking of the loom and shuttles shooting back and forth. Quilters work at their frames. In a studio a string quartet rehearses with characteristic bursts of intensity, and next door a lyric soprano is vocalizing, endlessly. A troupe of actors on a stage performs some- thing stark and dramatic with many interruptions and shouted suggestions from the director. On a small basement door I see a sign —Darkroom: No Admittance on Pain of Serious Personal Injury— a photographer is performing his arcane developing mysteries. On the attic level a novelist sits at a word processor staring into space, and a poet is determinedly at work on her thirty-seventh draft. Christ stands behind her, looking over her shoulder with interest.

In this house there is enough space for free movement between

the doings of body, mind, and soul. The sounds of conversation
and love, the music and rhythm of lives touched by lived-out realities, even the silence of a sleep-filled night, all wash into the artists'
creative consciousness. Some may ignore these signals, too busy to
attend. Others listen with welcoming ears, and it is their art that
bears the imprint of real life and the mystery that is its foundation.

And so the student, the marketing expert, the inventor, the carpenter, the computer programmer, the artist (all of whom show by
their presence in the house that they are part of the family) live in
the awareness of a reality joined to their own that has its center in
incarnation—God with us in Christ. T. S. Eliot put it, "When a
poet's mind is perfectly equipped for its work, it is constantly amal-
gamating disparate experiences"; so that in Eliot's examples, experiences such as falling in love and reading Spinoza, the noise of a
typewriter and the smell of cooking, come together into "new
wholes."

God's relationship with us surrounds us like a house. It is essential, the frame and backdrop for all thinking, doing, being. We
are at home in the divine presence in a way that is deeper than
consciousness.

The art of poets or musicians or novelists or actors or dancers
who are Christians is affected by the framework in which those
artists' visions appear—and out of which they create: a worldview
superintended by a living, loving, immanent deity and stocked

with images and values derived from him by way of the Word, the Spirit, and the family life of the Body.

Though the Christian artists' interior doors are open to what is going on in the household of faith, of which they are a part, their windows open on the universe. They do what they must do, finding and focusing their imaginations on a few of the infinite possibilities, most of which may have little or nothing to say formally or directly about their theology—which is the skeleton of the house in which they live and move and have their being.

Just as one may be unable, at any given moment, to determine whether or not a Christian is at prayer (the thoughts and intents of the heart are invisible, the body posture often indeterminate), so an artist's belief system may not be immediately discernible. We may need to examine a whole body of creative work, assembled over a lifetime, before attempting a judgment with regard to that poet's faith.

Artists effectively present biblical truth as metaphor, parable, analogy, poetry, vision, archetype, emblem, symbol, or story—artistry that has its roots in Scripture. Here truth is clothed with life, color, conflict—the textures of divine-human cooperation and achievement, human ingoddedness or rebellion, the drama of God's intervention and transformation. The word pictures of the Bible are imprinted indelibly on our minds, while what is abstract may easily escape us like evaporating mist.

If the gospel is foundational, out of it will naturally flow an art that does not deny its foundation but assumes it. If it is a given, we do not need to be reminded of its existence at every point. If our lives are centered in God's reality, we can risk working out from that center in new directions, each of which may hold the excitement of a fresh adventure.

And if the work of art truly reflects life experience, then it is itself a small facet of the truth of which Christ is author and communicator. This is the benison of the sacramental view of life: our realization that all of creation rightly belongs in the house of faith. Put another way, the Logos, which first called the universe into being, now embraces and defines it, assigning it meaning and value at every level. As C. S. Lewis said, "I believe in Christianity as I believe the Sun has risen not only because I see it but because by it I see everything else."[1]

It is in the complex fabric of natural and human life that God shines more clearly than in any abstract or dogmatic theological statement about him.

As Christians and artists, our ideas are derived not just from our own free-floating sensibilities and some accompanying aesthetic, but they have reference to a system of faith bigger than we are, with creation and gospel at its heart. Yet, with all the phenomena of the universe to write about, we are not free agents. Because we are residents in the house of faith, we are accountable to the community and its resident director and must shape our gift responsibly to perceive and penetrate to the heart of the matters we address, and to reveal their true shape and significance to the human community as well. As Christians, as artists, our work is radical, in the deepest sense of the word.

The road is rocky. One of its perils is that we may avoid giving voice to our most profound beliefs about Creator or creation for fear of disqualifying ourselves by appearing to preach or be overly pious, perhaps raising red flags in the minds of those who yet need to be convinced. Jeanne Murray Walker wrote to me, after the publication of her book of poems *Nailing Up the Home Sweet Home:*

You'll see when you read my book that I've tried to admit the whole scope of human emotion and subject matter into my work. Oddly enough, the danger of "evangelical diction" has made it very difficult for me to write straight-out, vibrant optimism, though of course that is what I often feel. I seem to be working the problem out in my own idiom. But I think this is a real roadblock for some young poets in the evangelical subculture.[2]

I find it fascinating to note that as we allow the created universe and the Scripture to illuminate us with their primary and secondary revelations, what we deeply believe will push up through the fabric of our writing or painting like green sprouts in spring, bursting the earth's crust.

When the artist lives in the house of faith, her or his consciousness is suffused with and informed by Christian images, and when that imaginative intelligence is allowed freely to describe life experience, the images and words supplied and shaped by the artist will reflect Christian belief even when there is no overt effort or intention to do so.

G. K. Chesterton said, "Nothing sublimely artistic has arisen out of mere art. . . . There must always be a rich, moral soil for any great artistic work." And so I become more aware of a number of correlations between faith and poetry. These *intersections*, as I call them, are elements of trusting God and making art not only as parallel to each other but as forming a network of connections that touch and interrupt, interlace and reinforce each other like the fibers in a woven fabric. For me poetry and faith are interdependent. *Each* affects the *other* as they embrace and interpenetrate. Faith informs art, and art enhances faith. They both, for each other, are breath for the bones.

This symbiosis is not surprising. For the Christian, both faith and art rest on a relationship with God and an acknowledgment of him as Source. If both come from God, both will explore and expose reality. But keen observation is essential, because the sum total of universal data is grist for their mills. In his Nobel lecture, poet Czeslaw Milosz said:

> One of the Nobel laureates of whom I read in childhood influenced . . . my notions of poetry. That was Selma Lagerlof. Her book *The Wonderful Adventures of Nils* places the hero in a double role. He is the one who flies above the earth and looks at it. This double vision may be a metaphor of the poet's vocation. He beholds under him rivers, lakes, forests; that is, a map, both distant and yet concrete. Hence, two attributes of the [artist]: avidity of the eye, and the desire to describe what he sees.[3]

Christian believers hear Jesus's cry echoing in their ears: "If your eye is single ["focused," author's rendering], your whole being will be full of light" (Matthew 6:22 NASB).

Because their source for understanding this multileveled reality is Spirit—invisible, yet powerfully residing in and shaping the universe—both artist and believer must occupy themselves with seeing what is virtually unseeable, what the earthbound miss. Like the servant of the beleaguered prophet Elijah, whose eyes were opened to see the host of the Lord surrounding them. Like the Saul-becoming-Paul, whose vision on the Damascus road was unseen by those who accompanied him. By alertness to clues and causes, by listening with inner ears, by opening the eyes of the heart to perceive what surges beneath, within, beyond, they begin to draw the ineffable into the realm of experienced reality.

Here belief is essential. What about "Seeing is believing"? Flannery O'Connor puts it this way: "For the writer, to believe nothing is to see nothing." Laurel Lee turned the old platitude around: "Some things have to be believed to be seen."

Anything may make us look: a breaking wave, a train whistle, a plummeting gull, an amorous couple. But art and the vision of faith allow us to *see*.

Such seeing demands concentration and persistence. Art and faith require not only perception but work. After the initial epiphany—the moment of revelation—come the fifty rough drafts, the struggle to enflesh the intangible, the wrestling match with the angel. And these are not for the fainthearted or lazy. Virginia Stem Owens exclaimed, "Pay attention? Attention is indeed the price we pay for awareness."

The most real and believable experience is personal, immediate, direct—knowing God is at work to shape me; me finding my own words, colors, idioms for what I am perceiving myself, fresh from the mind of God.

As artists and Christians, we also allow those we write for, speak to, or paint for the freedom to be part of the creative process of assimilating insight from our common Source.

Novelist and poet John Fowles said, "Fiction that is too tidy and finished . . . does not allow the reader an active enough role. It is much better to leave gaps which the reader will broach— one hopes."[4] Reading a novel or a poem or seeing a photograph or a play may be as imaginative a task as creating those things. Its significance comes from its ability to engage the imaginations of those who receive it, allowing them the creative latitude of interpretation.

The faith parallel is that each believer is to "work out [his or her] own salvation with fear and trembling" (Philippians 2:12 NKJV). As Christ assigns each a different task in the house of faith, each must perform the task with a unique set of gifts and graces that may change and develop with life and time.

Faith and art usually start small—this speaks to the two-pronged question of faith and art—a silken thread that joins unconnected phenomena, fine as a grain of mustard seed. Growing that given seed of trust in God, or art, requires the care and feeding of the imagination and the spirit. Both must be fertilized and cultivated.

My friend Pennie Thurman had horses. One fall in Illinois she gave me a cubic yard of horse manure for my vegetable garden. It was hard work to shovel it out of its container, spread it, dig it in. But after the labor was over, I could let the snow and rain soak its nutrients into the soil all winter. Next spring told the story in foot-long carrots and zucchini like green submarines.

It took work and time—the shifting seasons, day and night, heat and cold, just as faith and art take work and time. I know of no instant saints, no overnight artists. Yet if the horse manure of experience and concrete detail, gained by alert observation of God at work in our world, is allowed to soak into our consciousness throughout our years, we may harvest a nourishing imagery and an upward flowering of faith for souls and spirits within the household of faith.

And beyond it.

The Basics of Creativity:
Foundations of the Creative Process

Discovering the Creative Heart of God

Years ago, I was talking with my uncle Max, a hardworking, hard-bitten, shrewd, practical New Zealand apple farmer. Hearing that a new book of my poems had just been published, he asked me, with genuine bewilderment, "But—what *good* is a poem? What earthly use is it? Why can't you say what you want to say in a straightforward way that ordinary people can understand?"

At that moment, I was at a loss for words. How *do* you explain poetry—or any form of art or the creative process—to someone for whom it has no appeal, no meaning? Uncle Max's idea of art was probably summed up in the form of a well-pruned apple tree or a perfectly formed, ripe Cox's orange pippin, the hybridized apple for which his orchards were famous.

A few years and many internal debates later, I think I know how I could have answered him. I'd tell him that poetry, and any art, says something in a way that nothing else can, and that *something that art says* is so qualitatively different that it demands a radically different expression. Where linear, logical thinking may produce prose with a specific function—information or historical record or critical analysis or instruction—art selects and reflects on a small slice of human experience and lays it out there, a gift to anyone who is willing to savor it and enter into the artist's experience even in a minimal way. The artist, ideally, communicates experience in images and forms so precisely tailored, so personal, so multileveled that its insights go far beyond bare facts or mere *usefulness*.

David Jones, a British author, wrote:

> Man is a creature whose end is extra-mundane and whose nature
> is to make things and that the things made are not only things of
> mundane requirement but are of necessity the signs of something
> other. Further, that an element of the gratuitous adheres to this
> making.

It is true that much art has no practical use. While instructional prose may teach us how to approach a problem or outline the steps in developing a romantic relationship, the art in poetry is that it tells us cognitively what it feels like to have a sudden flash of understanding or to experience the wonder and exhilaration of being in love. It's my soul crying out to your soul: *This is what I see and how I feel. Can you see it? Can you feel it too?*

My uncle's questions apply to any art form: What good is it? What does it accomplish? Why does art even show up in the first

place? And for us as Christians, what is its significance? No matter what period of history or slice of international culture we
examine, we find human beings attempting to express beauty
and meaning—from the primitive figures scratched on Stone Age
cave walls to the sophisticated photography of Ansel Adams and
Galen Rowell.

Think of art's extraordinary diversity. It speaks from Aztec jew-
elry, Norse ballad, Indonesian batik, Russian folk dance, Inuit
Indian carving, as well as from Greek drama, Roman sculpture,
Gothic architecture, Oriental porcelain, the illuminated manu-
scripts of medieval monks, the baroque music of Bach and
Scarlatti, iridescent Venetian glass, Italian grand opera, the architecture of Le Corbusier; the paintings of Correggio, Rembrandt,
El Greco, and O'Keeffe. The decoration of human dwellings, artifacts, and bodies, and the elaboration of song and story are
graphic demonstrations of the human impulse that moves beyond
practical necessities toward something called beauty, which is further refined into art.

Alexsandr Solzhenitzyn, in his lecture on being awarded the
Nobel Prize for literature, said:

> Archeologists have not yet discovered any stage of human exis-
> tence without art. Even in the half-light before the dawn of
> humanity we received this gift from Hands we did not manage to
> discern. Nor have most of us managed to ask: Why was this gift
> given to us, and what are we to do with it?[1]

Art is what we say, what we sing, and what we show (in bodily
movement or the work of our hands) about what is bubbling up
within us, that which cries for recognition and response. Because it

seems so special, so wondrous, so extraordinary to us—this up-
welling from our creative imaginations—we want to share it with
kindred spirits. And so we have poetry readings and gallery exhibits
of art and concerts and square dances and films and fashion shows
and coffee-table books.

If we are honest, we all will admit that we have been moved
by such impulses from time to time. Especially when we are young,
we try to draw, to write a sonnet, to use finger paint, or to bake
a gingerbread man. We run and dance when we are too happy
simply to walk, or we sing and whistle when speaking is inade-
quate to express what we feel.

But why? Where do these impulses spring from? And why are
they so universal? For the Christian believer it is significant that
though we have been uniquely "made" by God, we sense that we
are not merely mechanisms whose sole purpose is to function
efficiently, sustaining our lives, performing mental and physical
work as part of our social infrastructure, and reproducing ourselves in an endless cycle of birth, growth, life, and death. We who
believe we bear God's image will realize how that image includes
the capacity to imagine and create, because God is himself an
imaginative Creator.

If we grant that as artists, our ways of creating and seeing begin
with the creativity of God, then let's look at the root of that imaginative impulse. What did the Creator have in mind when he spoke
our radiantly beautiful world into being? The magnificent ongoing
act of creation shows an astonishing kind of power and a breath-
taking kind of good.

Isaiah spoke prophetically about the creative power of God. Listen how he described the dynamic of God in creation (the word *dynamic* has its root in the Greek *dunamis*, from which we get explosive words like *dynamite*). God is "the Lord, who created the heavens and stretched them out, who spread out the earth and what comes from it, who gives breath to the people upon it and spirit to those who walk in it" (Isaiah 42:5 NRSV).

The one who created, who gave breath to every being, right at the beginning of the world, also made a garden—Eden. Every growing thing in it was designed and planted by God with purpose and faultless proportional balance and planning, climate control, a cycle of seasons, and systems of nourishment and growth and of adaptation and reproduction.

As artists we look to God's own creativity, beginning with his hand in nature, because nature is God's great revelation of himself, his richness, his complexity, his intelligence, his beauty, his mystery, his creativity, his great power and glory. The hints and clues to his nature are everywhere.

It has been said that God has written two books—the Book of Scripture and the Book of Nature. Next to my Bible, this is the realm where I experience God at work most powerfully. In fact, such an experience may be even more potent for me than the written Word because it is so immediate. I take it in firsthand, with all my senses. I am not just reading a story about wandering in the wilderness. I have wandered there myself, feeling fatigue and hunger as well as exuberance and wonder.

I read the apostle Paul's ecstatic hymn at the end of Romans 11:

> *Everything comes from him;*
> *Everything happens through him;*

Everything ends up in him.
Always glory! Always praise!
Yes. Yes. Yes. (Romans 11:36 MSG)

This has become my own song as well as Paul's. It is the credo of the *via affirmativa,* the life of celebration.

I believe God looks down on us—all of us—like an enthusiastic horticulturalist, as excited about us as he is about the infinite tonal shadings of green in the eucalyptus's narrow, saber-shaped leaves; that splash of apricot made by the Iceland poppies against the indigo lobelias; the way the tomatoes appreciate the marigolds for keeping away aphids; the Shasta daisies, like a bank of snow beyond the rose bushes; the way the sweet woodruff covers over the bare spots in the rock garden.

I imagine our Creator, an artist if there ever was one, beaming with happiness, loving all the varieties of growth and color, wild or tame, appreciating the wild Texas bluebonnets as much as the hybrid tea roses, and murmuring, "What a magnificent garden I've grown. Every plant unique and special. So much contrast! So much variety! How did I do it? I love them *all.*" And so I have to believe that uninterrupted nature, weeds and all, is divine art. It's not, as many of us assume, simply a "natural resource," a vast array of raw materials available for us to use for our own self-absorbed purposes.

Many fundamentalists have a stunted view of art as something nonessential; an option, perhaps, but not an important one. In so doing they ignore the gratuitous beauty (which means a gift of pure grace, quite undeserved) that the Creator included in creation, and the senses with which he endowed us so we can respond to that beauty. To have a functioning cosmos would have seemed enough. Beauty is an added bounty, and because the benefactor is divine, we ignore or disdain beauty at our peril, no matter where it is found.

Here the benison of the sacramental view of life is evident. As we read in the *Imitation of Christ*, "If your heart is straight with God, then every creature will be to you a mirror of life and a book of holy doctrine."[2] The created universe is crammed with pointers, clues to the nature and creatorship of this invisible Maker.

Even in the way the Scriptures are written—one-third of it in poetry, with vivid storytelling in the parables, and with even the most rigorous apostolic teaching illuminated by metaphor, analogy, and illustration—we receive an indication of the goodness of God in the vivid ways he informs the human imagination, that faculty of ours that sees pictures in our heads almost like colored slides projected on a screen.

God, who knows us better than we know ourselves, isn't content to speak simply to the rational intelligence but informs us through beauty, imagination, and intuition. Where doctrinal principles seem logical, though abstract, images print themselves on our minds and even on our senses in such brilliant color and three-dimensional texture that time and distraction cannot obliterate them.

In which order does God's hand work toward beauty and imagination? From the beginning the garden informed us, first order and then images. And then story. From the stories of Adam and Eve, to the histories of nations, to the story of incarnated God—all lead us to art.

And in the life of Jesus—the person of the Christ is the touchstone of the life and work of the Christian artist—we learn again from story. The parables of Jesus were not meant to be dissected analytically. They were designed to be taken in through the senses and the imagination—the windows of the soul—and *felt*, their subtext of ideal, principle, and theological truth absorbed almost unconsciously as the mental image suffuses the understanding over a period of time, a kind of divine soft-sell salesmanship. These are all the Creatorly ways that God chooses to come near to us and give us a window to his creative heart.

Responses to creation are the responses of an artist. That's how art comes into being, when there's a sudden excitement and exhilaration of spirit in simply observing and being part of that creation, seen in its daily detail and singularity.

These are artists of faith, whose vocation is to be cocreators (or at least sub-creators) with God, and who see themselves as made in his image and doing his will by calling attention to the design and beauty and diversity and strength and contrast and complexity of the created universe, which is ultimately an expression of the person of God.

The artist, then, becomes something of a prophet: the seer, the mouthpiece. The role of the artist is to *call to attention*. The question arises: Why is such an intermediary as an artist or a prophet often necessary for a divine message to be transmitted?

Why, at some points in faith and history, is the Word not spoken or seen directly, in its full blaze of light and sound and color and meaning, to the entire human community? Certain possibilities suggest themselves.

First, the difficulty of fragile, vulnerable humans faced with the God of glory. As Emily Dickinson succinctly phrased it: "The Truth must dazzle gradually / or every man be blind—"

My good friend Walter Hearn told me in a letter of a conversation with a Baptist colleague who had become a high church Anglican. Hearn remarked to his friend that he found all the liturgical apparatus distracting, that it got in the way of his direct experience of God. "Of course it does, you ninny!" his friend replied. "That's what it's there for. God is too glorious to be apprehended directly. The liturgy, the robes, the incense, the chanting are to enable you to stand in the presence of God without being bowled over by the power."

A full frontal view of the Almighty, swift as light, sharp and intense as a laser, with the energy of the universe flashing from his eyes, and with the earth and us on it, cradled like a marble in his palm, would paralyze, flatten, and annihilate us.

Yet here we are, hale and whole, and every day God shows us his goodness, just as he promised Moses. ["I will make all my goodness pass before you" (Exodus 33:19 NRSV).] Biblically, it is visible not only in the images God projects of himself (shepherd, mother hen, protective fortress, banner, evergreen tree) but also in the very fact that *they are pictures*. With Virginia Stem Owens, I ask, "Give me phenomena . . . Give me pictures and models . . . The one thing I cannot take is the denying darkness and the blind man's eye."

The artists—the prophets too—are called to this role: presenting pictures and models, words, and visions. They have a special calling—to recognize God's creating hand, God's storied art, God's order.

There is another calling for the artist, and that is one of linking earth to heaven, pointing the human to the divine, finding the connections. My father, a preacher by both calling and disposition, would often deliver this axiomatic advice to whoever happened to be listening: "Beware of being so heavenly minded that you're no earthly use."

I've never quite fallen into that trap; my inclinations tend to favor earthly mindedness. Nevertheless, both history and theology provide evidence of a discontinuity between the two states (of mind and/or spirit or reality), a lacuna that seems to demand exploration. If we are to stand within the framework of Christian belief, as artists and Christians, we are required to take both earth and heaven seriously; and, moreover, to attempt to find connections that bridge the gap between the two.

Learning to be amphibious, that is, adapting to life in these two radically divergent realms, heaven and earth, demands of us that we learn to see again through different lenses than those to which we have become accustomed.

Amphibian

Warm
after a while on a rock,
drunk with sky, her green silk
shrivels with wind. With a wet,
singular sound, then, she creases
the silver film, turns fluid,
her webbed toes accomplishing

the dark dive to water bottom and
the long soak, until her lungs,
spun for air, urge her up
for breath.
She moves
in two worlds, caught between
upper and under, never home.
Restless—skin withering for wet,
and the nether ooze,
or nostrils aching to fill
with free air her bubble lungs,
heart thumping, tympanum
throat pulsing to flood
the deepening sky with loud
frog song.[3]

Luci Shaw, *Polishing the*
Petoskey Stone

Sometimes I have seen myself as an amphibian, like a frog, created for two elements. I dive beneath the lake's surface, my earthly home, so that my skin doesn't dry out and wither, but I need oxygen for my lungs and have to emerge from below the surface to breathe. I discover that I am made for both earth and heaven.

Like Enoch, like Moses; unlike Adam, unlike most of us, these extraordinary individuals moved seamlessly from restricted terrestrial living into the presence of freedom and life in its optimum dimension in the presence of God.

And here *we* are, day by day attempting the utterly impossible. We are called to perform the rash absurdities of the redeemed or

to expire miserably. In effect Christ calls us to "perform impossi-
bilities or perish" like the fig tree that came under the curse of his
displeasure. Not only are we responsible as artists somehow to
demonstrate that it is possible to bring heaven to earth by living
the life of grace in an ungraceful place, by gluing together the
seen and the unseen, but we are required to be links with the
unlinkable, with otherwise disparate entities. As Arthur Koestler
said in *The Sleepwalkers*:

> It is a perverse mistake to identify the religious need solely with
> intuition and emotion, science solely with the logical and rational.
> Prophets and discoverers, painters and poets all share this amphib-
> ial quality of living both in the contoured drylands and in the
> boundless ocean.[4]

As artists, especially, some of us have experienced, as Paul the
apostle did, a carrying into the third heaven; we have been off
guard enough to be swept from our pedestrian stance, to have
grown wings, or to be quite suddenly able to walk on water, blood
surging, the light we move into so different from ordinary daylight, so bright around us that we are burned, aware that grace has
seized and carried us away. The word *rapture* is appropriate. (I'm
reminded of my high school definition of the Latin *rapio*—"to
seize and carry off to a state in which everything is changed.")

But the moment ebbs away. The epiphany is snuffed out like a
candle. Once again we are on an earth imperturbably solid and
unyielding, and we are back to groping in shadow again. Seeing
only through a glass, darkly. Despite this groping, creativity's call
is to find that way to tell, to show, to sing, to paint epiphany—at
least to attempt what was seen in the third heaven or what is

hoped for despite the darkening glass—even on this solid and unyielding earth.

As artists, what we look for in making the connections, what we need, and what the Holy Spirit gave in inspiring the biblical writers are images that work. The more effective and varied the images, the more levels of truth and illumination they provide. We need multiplicity; the more images the better, not mixed but compounded. What one image fails to recognize, another will pick up, like the reflection seen in different facets of a gem as it is turned in the light.

There is a kind of "safety in numbers" here: the more we surround ourselves with reflective, connotative images, the more perfectly we will see "the whole picture." Robert Farrar Capon commented that "the great thing about Scripture is the images it gives you . . . a thousand flashlights of different colors and intensities. Scripture is a box full of flashlights, and the role of theology [or art, I would add] is to take these flashlights and play with them."[5]

This is what I want to say to fellow artists: in looking at our tools we have for our art—words, colors, motion, breath, song, clay—we notice that God has used the things of this earth, of story, of picture, of detail. Here is how we look at God's transformation of meaning through method. As God took Abraham and made him a picture of faith, so, down through history, he has taken other human beings and made of them living art—to convey his messages in effective and dramatic ways.

And in the Incarnation, Christ became a living Word. Jesus took the risk of reducing himself to what we could see and touch and listen to, a living message that bridged the huge communication gap between deity and humankind. The person, the Word that is Christ, is the touchstone of the life and work of the Christian artist.

Jesus, as the Logos, who first called the universe into being, now embraces and defines it, assigning it meaning and value at every level. Take this poem, "Christmas, Whidbey Island," by my Regent College colleague Loren Wilkinson:

> *Not in the waves, not in the wave torn kelp;*
> *Not in the heron by the lake at dawn*
> *Nor owls' haunting of the wood,*
> *Nor rabbits browsing frightened on the lawn;*
> *Neither in the widening whirl*
> *Of seashell, galaxy, or cedar burl,*
> *Nor in the mushrooms' bursting of the humid ground*
> *May God the fathering be found,*
>
> *If not found first in Bethlehem,*
> *In thistly hay, on hoof-packed earth,*
> *Where a girl, cruciform with pain*
> *Grips manger boards in child birth.*
> *There in the harsh particular,*
> *In drafts, and stench of cow manure*
> *The squalls of Christ, Creator, sound;*
> *Where God grasped not at Godhead in a child*
> *There only will the God of life be found.*
>
> *Now, if we upon this wave-shaped bluff*
> *Stand in the straw of Bethlehem*

Then God shines out from everything:
The agate in the surf, the withered flower stem,
The fish that gives its body for the seal,
The flesh, the fruits that form each common meal,
The dance of pain and love in which our lives are wound;
Since Christ was flesh at Bethlehem,
*In all the world's flesh may God be found.*⁶

With Wilkinson, we find the cosmic center of all beauty and meaning is to be found in Bethlehem, site of the Incarnation, flashpoint of the joining of heaven and earth, invisible and visible reality, transcendent and material. And it is in the "harsh particular" of earthy detail and the complex fabric of nature and humanity that God shines out more clearly than in any abstract formulations or theological constructs about him.

Incarnation shows us simply, clearly, what otherwise would have blinded us—Jesus, Logos, metaphor of God, Word that shows and tells, accessible yet mysterious, essence as well as sacrament, actuality and analogy both. As we become accountable to him, we learn to shape our gifts responsibly to penetrate to the heart of matters, to eschew mere surfaces, to find and celebrate both immutability and growth, and we are forced to be radical in the deepest sense of the word.

We who believe we bear God's image realize how that image includes the capacity to imagine and create, because God is himself an imaginative Creator. Though we cannot produce something out of nothing, as God did, we can combine the elements and forms available to us in striking and original ways that arise out of the unique human ability (designed and built into us by God) to imagine, to *see pictures in our heads*. And beyond that, to remember things from our past that no longer exist and mentally to invent things that have as yet no reality, to hear sounds and rhythms and recognize patterns and to translate them into forms that will strike a chord in the hearts of other human beings. In art and creativity, we make visible to others the beauty and meaning God has first pictured, or introduced, into our imaginations. In that sense we may each think of ourselves as a small extension of the creative mind of God.

I take as my mandate as a writer the divine word to John on Patmos: "Fear not; write what you see" (Revelation 1:19, author's rendering). As we write the truth about what we see, in all its concrete detail, its hard and shining edges, or its faintly glimpsed outlines seen through mist, the correspondences will make themselves known to us. In the process of writing or making art, or being prophets, we are peeling back the layers, unearthing the universe to its heart. We are also continuing the work of creation; as we see pictures in our heads and translate them into a new kind of reality, we are demonstrating that we are made in the image of one who saw a whole universe in his mind—and created it.

Chapter Two

Entering into Beauty

There is nothing in the universe about which art cannot be created. For me, art is in the impulse that gathers materials from our disparate but rich and compellingly diverse environment and assembles them in a way that brings a kind of order out of their chaos, an order with elements of both conflict and resolution.

Art is also the result of our human impulse to find expression for that something within us that responds to the stimuli surrounding us, crying out to be expressed, to find meaning in beauty, or terror, or sex, or something as mundane as food, and to reflect this in a form, a medium that produces a response—awe, excitement, disgust, wonder, even shock or anger—in those around us.

This aesthetic impulse seems to be universal. Art finds meaning in all of human experience or endeavor, drawing from it strength and surprise by reminding us of what we know but may never have truly recognized before, transcending our particularity with soaring ease.

There is no society on earth that does not attempt to decorate or embellish or enhance its dwelling places, its garments, its artifacts, its language, or the human body itself—either with graphic design or fabric or song or word or ritual. Maybe art and religion are aligned because religion also addresses the world in its attempt to seek and find, knock, and trust that God will open the door to truth, beauty, and the meaning of our living.

Art lays bare our realities. And religion opens our experience up to God. Think of the wonderful iconography of the Greek and Russian Orthodox communities. Think of the way Native American art and animistic African art mirror their belief systems. Recollect Christian church structure with its cross-shaped nave and transept, its wealth of sign and symbol and story in stained glass, stone and wood carving, and the very design of the church building itself (called in preliterate society "the poor people's Bible" because it filled the heart and mind with images and colors and shapes that spoke of divine realities). Art was seen in medieval and Renaissance painting and sculpture and music as a vehicle for expressing the glory of God. In the baroque era, composers such as Bach made notations on their musical scores: *Soli gloria deo* (Glory to God alone). Art and religion were truly married.

With the Enlightenment, art and religion began to split apart in European and Western culture, so that even a poet as deeply in tune with the natural and supernatural worlds as Gerard Manley Hopkins responded to that cultural divide and felt compelled to burn his early work, a personal sacrifice to God he labeled "the slaughter of the innocents." For seven years thereafter Hopkins rigorously disciplined himself, attempting in his priestly role to worship and serve God apart from poetry, until one day his religious superior hinted in his hearing that "someone" ought to write a poem about the wreck of the ship the *Deutschland*—which spurred Hopkins's poetry career anew, as well as reintroducing him to the necessary, God-ordained marriage of the life of art and the life of faith.

Again, to the question my uncle Max, the apple farmer, asked about what service art performs: in our created universe pure functionality might seem to be enough to fulfill God's creative purpose. So we ask along with Uncle Max, "How essential is beauty to the working of the universe?" Philosophers and metaphysicians may disagree about this, though surprisingly "elegance" is something that today's scientists strive for in their theories and equations. It seems that the inclusion of the desire and appreciation for the beautiful is gratuitous—an infusion of pure grace, a reflection of the generous heart of the Creator.

When we create something appealing, even in an act as pragmatic as the way we arrange our living rooms and choose the color of the wallpaper, or add a new typeface to our printer fonts, we show our integral relationship with the Creator. God, the first quilter of prairies, the prime painter (sunsets, thunderheads, forget-me-nots), the archetypal metal sculptor (mountain ranges, crystalline structures), the composer who heard birdsongs and the whales' strange, sonorous clickings and croonings in his head long before

there were birds or whales to sing them, the poet whose Word
was "full of grace and truth" (John 1:14 NRSV)—translated his own
divine image in our human flesh so that we too are participants in
creative intelligence and originality.

So we see that beauty is the business of the artist as we seek to
create in the image of the Creator. But it is also the delight of
every ordinary human being, because we are all created, in God's
image, to create. Have you ever heard of *anyone* who has not, at
some point in his or her life, yielded to the creative impulse?
Doodled? Decorated an Easter egg or a Christmas tree? Land-
scaped a garden plot? Written a poem or a song for the guitar to
the object of their affections? And didn't you, as you got dressed
this very morning—*you, getting dressed, this morning*—pay some
attention not only to being warm and comfortable and decently
covered, but also, to some degree, attractive? We care how we
look. And it is not just part of the human mating ritual. It is
because appearances often reflect something deeper—something
about who we are. Beauty matters.

When you move into a new home or apartment, don't you
make some effort to make the color scheme, the wallpaper, the
arrangement of furniture pleasing? Even in your office, you'll
bring in a potted plant and a pictorial calendar or poster to add
some life and color to an otherwise drab cubicle.

Beauty is integral, so deeply a part of who we are and what we
enjoy that we may take it for granted. Even flawed or marred or dis-
torted as a result of human depravity and failure, it is still visible in
the fingerprints of the Creator on the natural world.

Beauty is perhaps one of the few things that *constantly calls us
back to God*, that reminds us of an ideal of goodness and vitality, a
reality that embodies the beautiful. The Benedictines hold that

beauty is "truth shining into being," a principle adopted by John Keats in his famous "beauty is truth, truth beauty." In this sense beauty is redemptive. It can motivate us to turn a corner, to pursue a new objective. It awakens us because it is often so surprising.

Beauty is always tied to the real, the observable. It is there to be seen. Heard. Imagined. Experienced. Celebrated.

Universally, beauty gives pleasure. It awakens sensations that may have lain dormant. It arrives through the windows of our souls, our five senses—hearing (music, the small sounds of the rain forest, drum rhythms), sight (landscapes, colors, textures, contrasts—which is why my photography is so stimulating for me), touch (the nerves of our fingers are tuned to smooth, rough, silky, oily, warm, chilled, frosty), taste (cinnamon rolls, good coffee, vintage wine, toffee, mint jelly, roast beef with horseradish and Yorkshire pudding), or smell (roses, bread bak-ing, Chanel No. 5, newly cut grass, etc.). The messages of beauty through the senses, when combined with reasoning intelligence, achieve meaning or significance for us. They lodge in our minds and memories and do their transforming work in us, reminding us of the one behind the messages.

I have vowed never to cut myself off from beauty. Dallas Willard counsels us to "cultivate the beautiful." For me it is God's grace in action, the invisible made visible, the Word made flesh and dwelling with me, grace in glorious three-dimensional color with better-than-Dolby sound; and fragrance, taste, and texture thrown in to make it even more memorable.

Though beauty is personal, in individuals with differing tastes and standards, I love to think of beauty's universality. Around the globe we all gasp at the sight of wild breakers sending up violent white foam as they crash on the coastal rocks. We breathe in the silent greenness of field and forest with their moist fragrances. The icy blue of icebergs in the Antarctic. The subtle earth tones of the painted deserts of Arizona and New Mexico and the Kalahari. We call our friends on the phone to witness with us the golden glory of the sun setting behind spectacular purple clouds. (This happened to me just the other day.)

And *sunrises!*

Turning to music, think of its infinite variety of possibilities. Mozart is beautiful, and Palestrina and Respighi and John Rutter. (Add your own favorites to this list.) Bach is beautiful. Part of Bach's beauty for me is that it is linked to his celebration of the Creator's work and worth, celebrating order and beauty and meaning—God-work, in which we are cocreators.

Yes, beauty matters. It is important to God. Why else would he shape and color fish, birds, insects, rocks, plants, and people with such rich diversity? As my friend Elizabeth Rooney once said, "Imagine making something as useful as a tree, as efficient at converting sunlight into food and fuel, as huge and tough as a white oak that can live three hundred years, and then decorating it in spring with tiny pink leaves and pale green tassels of blossoms."

Beyond his primary creation of our vividly beautiful universe, with all its sounds and colors and smells and textures, God also seems to be interested in helping his people create and appreciate beauty. One example in which human beings reflect or imitate

God's own love for the beautiful, and in which they cocreate with the Creator, is seen in Exodus 31:1–11.

> GOD spoke to Moses: "See what I've done; I've personally chosen Bezalel son of Uri, son of Hur of the tribe of Judah. I've filled him with the Spirit of God, giving him skill and know-how and expertise in every kind of craft to create designs and work in gold, silver, and bronze; to cut and set gemstones; to carve wood—he's an all-around craftsman.
>
> "Not only that, but I've given him Oholiab, son of Ahisamach of the tribe of Dan, to work with him. And to all who have an aptitude for crafts I've given the skills to make all the things I've commanded you: the Tent of Meeting, the Chest of The Testimony and its Atonement-Cover, all the implements for the Tent, the Table and its implements, the pure Lampstand and all its implements, the Altar of Incense, the Altar of Whole-Burnt-Offering and all its implements, the Washbasin and its base, the official vestments, the holy vestments for Aaron the priest and his sons in their priestly duties, the anointing oil, and the aromatic incense for the Holy Place—they'll make everything just the way I've commanded you." (MSG)

Here Bezalel's intelligent craftsmanship and his ability in design are said to be the direct results of his in-filling by the Spirit of God. Spirit-filled Bezalel and his helper, Oholiab, also gifted with, as it says in Exodus 35:35, "ability to do every sort of work done by a craftsman or . . . skilled designer" (RSV), are models for artist Christians today.

Biblical models for aesthetic detail and creative skills in implementing them are numerous. Note Jehovah's instructions in an earlier chapter of Exodus: "You shall make the robe of the ephod all of blue. . . . You shall make on its hem pomegranates of blue and purple and scarlet material . . . and bells of gold between them" (Exodus 28:31, 33 NASB). Pattern, color, and sound all at work together.

God also introduced elements of abstract art (that is, of pure design) into the temple, as well as representational and symbolic art. Consider the two intricately ornamented bronze pillars set up in its vestibule. As Francis Schaeffer commented in *Art and the Bible:* "They supported no architectural weight and had no utilitarian engineering significance. They were there only because God said they should be there as a thing of beauty."[1]

The attention God gives to beauty and to the illumination that comes through art is not confined to physical decoration. By his consistent use of imagery throughout the Bible For example, "He will be like a tree planted . . ." (Jeremiah 17:8 NIV); "As the deer pants for the water brooks . . ." (Psalms 42:1 NKJV); "The fields are white for harvest" (John 4:35 ESV); " 'The tongue is a fire" (James 3:6 NKJV). God sets his seal of approval on an imaginative mode for thinking and expressing truth. Thousands of richly inventive figures of speech demonstrate how God thinks and that he speaks in pictures as well as propositions. Instead of talking abstractly about divine power to forgive sinners, here's how the prophet (in Isaiah 1:18) expresses the same idea in imagery: "Though your sins are as scarlet, they will be as white as snow; though they are red like crimson, they will be like wool." These are words that imprint themselves in our imaginations through their reference to color and texture.

God welcomes the beauty of performing arts: singing (1

Chronicles 15), dancing (2 Samuel 6 and Psalm 149), and instrumental music (1 Chronicles 23 and Psalm 150), among many
other references. Gene Edward Veith observes in *The Gift of Art*
that "nearly the whole range of the arts can be found in God's
Word"—the visual arts and music, literary art, poetry in the
Psalms, fiction in the parables, and drama in the street theater of
the prophets.

Art and the appreciation of beauty are thus solidly rooted in
God's creation and communication to us. For Christians to shun,
fear, or condemn the arts seems as anti-God as atheism. The creative imagination as expressed in the arts can glorify God and illuminate the human spirit with his truth. Dr. John Walford, an art
historian trained at Cambridge University, says, "The arts are
parts of God's provision for our human well-being. The more
these elements are absent from our lives, the more we are alien-
ated from the fullness of life as provided by God."[2]

For artists, the fullness (indeed the necessity) that art brings to our
lives is the impulse that results in our longing toward God, toward
beauty, no matter what the circumstances of our lives; it comes
into our daily striving.

In an article about life on the prairies, I read about a Canadian
prairie woman who in 1870 wrote in her diary a note about her
quiltmaking: "I make them warm to keep my family from freez-
ing; I make them beautiful to keep my heart from breaking." To
construct a quilt is to make beauty and meaning out of life's
scrappy leftovers. The image in that wry entry is powerful.

Quiltmaker

To keep a husband and five children warm,
she quilts them covers thick as drifts against
the door. Through every fleshy square white threads
needle their almost invisible tracks; her hours
count each small suture that holds together
the raw-cut, uncolored edges of her life.
She pieces each one beautiful, and summer bright
to thaw her frozen soul. Under her fingers
the scraps grow to green birds and purple
improbable leaves; deeper than calico, her mid-winter
mind bursts into flowers. She watches them unfold
between the double stars, the wedding rings.[3]

Luci Shaw, *Polishing the*
Petoskey Stone

And sometimes beauty does feel like a matter of survival. The drab can be deadly; without beauty a part of us dies. Frederick Buechner said of beauty: "It is to the spirit what food is to the flesh. It fills an emptiness in you that nothing else under the sun can."

When the world was created, it would have been enough to have it *work*, wouldn't it? To include beauty seems gratuitous, a gift of pure grace, which I believe it is. Our own creation of beauty links us with our Creator. God was the first quilter of wood and prairie landscapes; the prime painter of night skies, ferns, snow on cedars; the sculptor of icebergs and rock formations; the composer of sounds as varied as wind moaning and water's loud pulsing in ferocity against the shore's sands; the play-wright who plotted the sweeping drama of creation, Incarnation, redemption; and the poet whose Word said it all.

God made humans in his image; we participate in creative intelligence, giftedness, originality. We all have the faculty of imagination deep within us, waiting, like a seed to be watered and fertilized. Imagination gives us pictures by which to see things the way they *can* be, or the way they *are* underneath.

The prairie woman, hemmed in with her small children by months of subzero cold and snow, used her imagination redemptively. Around the traditional quilt patterns—double stars, wedding rings—her imagination pieced in the exuberant flowers and leaves that redeemed the long winter, which thawed her soul. She created beauty and richness from the ordinary stuff, even the cast-offs, the old colored rags of her life.

At that point, in that redemptive action of the winter quilt, beauty becomes sacramental, pointing beyond itself to something even larger, truer, more potent. As Eugene Peterson says in *Leap Over a Wall*:

> There's a long tradition in the Christian life, most developed in Eastern Orthodoxy, of honoring beauty as a witness to God and a call to prayer. Beauty is never only what our senses report to us but always also a sign of what's just beyond our senses—an inner-ness and depth. There's more to beauty than we can account for empirically. In that more and beyond, we discern God. Artists who wake up our jaded senses and help us attend to these matters are gospel evangelists.

Peterson adds:

In the presence of the beautiful we intuitively respond in delight,
wanting to be involved, getting near, entering in—tapping our feet,
humming along, touching, kissing, meditating, contemplating,
imitating, believing, praying. It's the very nature of our five senses
to pull us into whatever is there—scent, rhythm, texture, vision.
And it's the vocation of the artist to activate our senses so that they
do just that. Beauty in bird and flower, in rock and cloud. Beauty in
ocean and mountain, in star and sand. Beauty in storm and
meadow, in laughter and play. But most exquisitely beauty in the
human body, with its fulfillment in the human face. Instinctively .
. . we recognize that there's more to beauty than what we discern
with our senses. That beauty is never "skin deep," but always reve-
latory of goodness and truth. Beauty releases light into our awareness so that we're conscious of the beauty of the Lord.[4]

And it is then that we can worship the Lord "in the beauty of
holiness."

I like what Peterson says about the beauty of the human face.
It reminds me of Emerson's quote: "We ascribe beauty to that
which is simple, which has no superfluous parts; which exactly
answers its end." At that point beauty and function are joined.
Which is, I suspect, what God intended all along. But the simplicity that Emerson commended is not quite as simple as he made
out. Beauty is also rich and diverse, appearing in different guises
to different people.

I'm an Episcopalian, so I belong to a church where the arts are
celebrated and appreciated. But for some churches, if you're not

actively evangelizing, "saving souls," you're not in the business of God. To me, the business of God is to be as fully human as God programmed us to be. And that includes the creative impulse, the impulse toward beauty as well as the witness of a life lived well.

The Episcopal way of worship, I have found—with its sacramental interpretation of life, its richness of sign and symbol—speaks to my imagination and awakens a fresh inner reaction. At first it was just one unexpected epiphany after another, but now, after twenty years, it has become second nature—the vocal responses, the easy movement from knees to pew to standing to altar, the passing of the peace, the genuflection toward the cross and the altar, and the crossing of oneself to signal the blessings of grace from Father, Son, and Spirit. To me—beauty.

The Episcopal Church provides sign and symbol—even incense, which many Protestants might find excessively ecclesiastical, but which is to me a beautiful visual image of faith. The pungent aroma instantly speaks to my spirit—"Prayer rising to God," as Psalm 141:1–2 suggests, with its words, "God, come close . . . Treat my prayer as sweet incense rising" (MSG).

In the Communion service I love the progression from the Liturgy of the Word, with its tying together of Scripture from Old and New Testaments, the Psalms, the Gospels. As we read Scripture and hear it expounded, as we are confronted with its truth, we confess our sins, we pray for cleansing, and we receive the assurance that God has forgiven us. And then we move into the Liturgy of the Table, where we worship God in receiving the sacrament of Communion, the bread and the wine, the body and the blood of Christ. The bread and wine press a tender consciousness of Christ's enfleshment into my heart. These moments, in the intimacy of the body of Christ, are what hold me in faith and in beauty. They call me to mystery and godhead.

The "show and tell" of the liturgical service is not just talking *about* something, *about* God or about his attributes, or *about* truth from Scripture. It actually enacts the mystery. Along with priests and deacons and lay ministers, the whole congregation is involved in worship. There are congregational responses, both in prayer and in Scripture. The whole thing is antiphonal. A dialogue is going on.

For me this is the high point of any week, as if my sense of God's presence there rises to a peak that sometimes is almost too strong and too poignant to describe. If I miss Communion for a week, I feel spiritually impoverished, undernourished. And as a writer, too, that's a lack I cannot bear; it affects the deepest levels of my life and work and speaks to me so clearly of the spiritual necessity of beauty.

I have a vision for the Church and art: I would love to see art and beauty embraced and acknowledged and not simply viewed as peripheral, nor as one option among many. I'd like to see art as central to the enriched Christian life.

For instance, liturgical dance is a wonderful way of seeing Scripture embodied; it's like praying with the bones and giving breath to the bones. In worship you may see a biblical event or response enfleshed in the human body in dance. Some churches now have a Saturday evening service, called *Sabado Primo,* the first Saturday of every month. It's an alternative service that allows for creative freedom, though it follows the liturgy of the Church in the sense that it's the Liturgy of the Word and the Table. Scripture can be dramatically presented, not simply as a reading. And at the time of the Eucharist, a simple dance around the table and the passing of the bread and wine to each other is a beautiful outworking of the community of Christ, the community of saints being together and celebrating.

No matter what our faith tradition, as artists we seek out the beautiful, the complex, in a house of worship. The architecture of any church can be either beautiful in ornamentation or plain and quiet in its beauty, as in the Brethren or Quaker traditions. Of course, our sense of beauty and aesthetics can be subjective, but if we come at it with a sense of creating sacred space that is appealing and worshipful, that glorifies and enriches the hearts of the people who gather there, I believe we please the heart of God.

All of us—people of faith, artists—see that beauty in the very actions of creation can be both simple and rich. Each of us is called to cultivate beauty, knowing that as artists, and as those with whom we share our creative gifts, we become more whole and healed in that sharing of beauty.

We do not need to be overwhelmed by the calling, as though attending to beauty in our lives and in our churches were something other than what God's very creation has called us toward. Begin as the quilter began, creating for both function and beauty. Perhaps we could *survive* without beauty—many people seem to. But the appreciation of beauty is almost like a muscle; if it isn't used, it becomes weakened and withers away.

We are each, in the image of our Creator, created to create, to call others back to beauty and holiness and to the truth about God's nature. We are each created to stop and cry to someone preoccupied or distracted with the superficial, "Look!" or "Listen!"

when, in something beautiful and meaningful, we hear a message from beyond us. Together, then, we may worship in holiness our Creator who, in his unlimited grace, calls us to become cocreators of beauty.

Chapter Three

Meeting the God of Metaphor

Twenty-one years ago, my husband of thirty-three years, who was also my best friend, died of lung cancer. During the time of coping and grieving and searching and reorientation, an incident occurred that has clarified my thinking and flooded my imagination. It has condensed itself into this brief parable, which starts out with phrases from the book of the prophet Isaiah: "The spirit of the Sovereign LORD is on me . . . to comfort all who mourn, and provide for those who grieve . . . beauty instead of ashes, the oil of gladness instead of mourning, and a garment of praise instead of a spirit of despair" (61:1–3).

After Harold died, my good friend Bernie Bosch and his sons took down the old, dead oak tree that stood in our front yard. The previous spring it had not leafed out at all, and we had known it must be toppled. Bernie waited until the ground was frozen hard so that the crash of its enormous bulk wouldn't damage the lawn.

It was a huge job. And after the screaming power saws were silent and the tree was dismembered, all the wood had to be split and trucked away (that was the deal—he cut the tree down in return for the wood), and the mass of debris piled on top of the stump and ignited. The white-hot blaze burned for days, and even after the flames died down, a thin tendril of smoke still threaded the air above the site. It looked like a dormant volcano. The fire ate away most of the stump and the roots deep below the surface so that a week later all that was left was a black-rimmed saucer of ashes like a wound in the sod.

It was then I realized why the felling of the tree occupied my thoughts so consistently and with such a sense of significance. It was because *I* was the frozen sod with the deep wound, and Harold was my tree who was simply . . . gone. How unreal it seemed that his roots, that had for more than thirty years penetrated deep into my life, that had anchored us and joined us so solidly and securely, had been eroded by the fire of decay. The space above ground that for so long had been filled with his vertical strength and solidity and shape was empty; air had rushed in where, before, the towering trunk had outbranched to leaves.

I waited for the tissue of earth and the skin of sod—the beauty of green instead of the gray ashes of a spent fire—to fill in and heal over the naked scar. And it did. It did. But the oak tree stands strong and thriving and leafy in my memory, and no one can cut it down.

Somehow, as I was thinking about Harold and the shape of our relationship, and the looming desolation of his loss, I needed something more than an abstract truth to latch on to. It wasn't enough for me to say, "Harold's gone. How I miss him! Now I must come to terms with life without him." I needed to find a picture, something so real in my imagination that I could derive sense impressions from it, and building from those stimuli I could perhaps see a pattern and derive significance from the image.

A metaphor. A metaphor, because of its implicit reality and force in one arena of life, can transfer or carry over its meaning into another arena. The image acts to bring sense and immediacy and relevance to the real-life situation it parallels.

Though many are not aware of it—even as those in the visual arts are quite keenly attuned to this—we think in pictures. Our imaginations are like screens on which are projected a series of color images. In her book about the process of creation, *The Mind of the Maker,* Dorothy Sayers states categorically that "we have no way to think, except in pictures."

In his book *The Mind of Jesus*, William Barclay suggests a reason for Jesus's use of parabolic imagery:

> When Jesus used the parable, he was using the method of teaching which all of us know from childhood. . . . To teach in parables is to teach in pictures. . . . Very few people are capable of grasping a purely abstract truth. . . . We might labor long and ineffectively to define the abstract idea of beauty, but if we can point to a person and say, "That is a beautiful person!" then the abstract idea becomes clearer.
>
> It is not only the Word which must become flesh. . . . Every great word must become a person before [we] can grasp and understand

it. So, when Paul speaks about faith, he does not enter into a long and abstract discussion and definition, he draws a living picture of Abraham. In Abraham, faith becomes flesh, the abstract becomes concrete, the idea becomes a picture and a person.[1]

C. S. Lewis points out our limitations in the face of imponderables:

Five senses, an incurably abstract intellect, a haphazardly selective memory, a set of preconceptions and assumptions so numerous that I can never examine more than a minority of them—never become conscious of them all. How much of total reality can such an apparatus let through?[2]

Limited as we are in our rational understanding and our ability to communicate meanings, we can, as Lewis pointed out, "neither apprehend Reality absolutely nor express ourselves exactly. Out of epistemological and semantic necessity we turn to metaphor. . . . We can make our language duller; we cannot make it less metaphorical."[3]

George MacDonald's words echo a similar conviction: "How can we speak of these things at all if we speak not in figures?" The unseeable, the ineffable, the transcendent must be narrowed, gentled, solidified, contained in metaphors or we could not survive. And this is one reason for the consistent use of imagery throughout the Bible.

There is, of course, a theological school of thought that tries to get at truth abstractly, without the use of metaphor. Carl F. Henry, for instance, states, "Truth is only propositional/verbal." The logic of such a statement seems to go like this: Brief is beautiful. We're looking for some cogent, lucid, linear logic that ends all discussion, that says it all, that is so immensely powerful that it captures and condenses thought into "pure truth."

And this is an honorable search.

I am not, nor ever will be, a scientist, but my doctor son, John, a science major during his college years, contributed this information to the following discussion: In the world of chemistry the process of purification often involves condensation. That is, if some substance has been dissolved in water and all we want is that original substance, we can isolate it again by heating the solution to the boiling point and evaporating the water.

Unfortunately, this doesn't always work. There are substances that, when mixed with water or any solvent, form solutions called *azeotropes* that cannot be separated by boiling; their constituent elements are chemically bound.

My point is that there seem to be two kinds of truth. One kind can be condensed out from all additives and made pure and potent, like the simple but profound *elegance* (the word loved by scientists) of Einstein's $E=mc^2$. Another kind, an "azeotropic" truth, if you will, is bound to imagery; it cannot be condensed into a simple propositional statement.

A principle, a proposition, a formula, even a systematic theology, tends to gather things together and then smooth them out again, ignoring minor inconsistencies, overlooking exceptions. The general systematic statement about reality, whether in science or theology, has much the same effect on us as a view of the earth from a satellite or the topography found in a map. It may supply us with certain otherwise unobtainable information, gnomic in nature. But if we soon lose interest, it is because much of the detail has been lost.

Where proposition truth twirls the table model of the globe, imagination focuses on the single blade of grass, on the grain of wood in a floorboard, on the helical unfolding of a shell, or on the spears of frost across a window. This is where the artist, the writer, finds a way through to understanding—in the pictures, the details.

Truth is a touchy topic, a daunting word. It sounds so *ultimate,* so solemn, with nothing whimsical or casual about it, so that we cannot joke about it without feeling uneasy. It demands our serious thought, our total commitment—and still we're baffled by it. After all, thinking people have been searching for truth for eons, and it has proved eternally elusive, defying definition.

Although its shape escapes us, we sense its relation to the way things *really are,* actuality beyond mere fact, the core, the root of things, the rock bottom of reality.

Notice how, to get at a definition of truth, we are forced to use metaphors like *core, root, rock, bottom.* Because of its disconcerting abstraction, its largeness and inscrutability, we must choose symbols to make it seem more manageable, more concrete, more complete, more than simply propositional.

At this point the artist, the writer, the playwright may ask why we are beginning the conversation about art with a conversation about truth. Perhaps because artists are asking questions of truth, and understand that in taking truth to another level, we meet *paradox*: an example of the kind of multifaceted truth that baffles the propositionalist (trying in vain to reduce it to a formulaic abstraction) and delights the poet (in whose imagination it is bound to analogies and images). Paradox is something that artists know well. For the prophet Isaiah to use *oaks* as a metaphor for his text, about those who "will be called oaks of righteousness, the planting of the Lord"(61:3 NRSV), and elsewhere to describe them as grass, is paradox. It is paradoxical for me to think of my late husband in terms of the toughness and height and strength and durability of an oak tree and yet realize that he also partook of grass's tenderness, transience, and vulnerability.

For artists to live with paradox, to think and act in a world permeated with paradox, we must learn to view life metaphorically. Poet William Stafford said it so well:

> So, the world happens twice—
> once what we see it as,
> second, it legends itself
> Deep, the way it is.[4]

This metaphorical view sees the world not as reducible to verbal proposition but as multileveled, complex, rich, its mystery capable only of being pierced and presented as imagery. The key word in Stafford's stanza is *legend*—used as a verb it points the alternate, authentic track to truth through myth, story, imagery, metaphor.

Thomas Howard furthered the idea:

It is in the nature of things to appear in images—royalty in lions and kings, strength in bulls and heroes, terror in oceans and thunder. . . . The inclination to trace correspondences among things transfigures those things into images of one another so that on all levels it is felt that *this suggests that*.[5]

In this view the multiple interconnecting links throughout the universe are not random. They are like a finely spun web, a fabric woven with purpose by a God "in whom all things hold together." It is in this world, these levels, these links, that the artist lives and works.

The propositional and the metaphorical approaches—these two flight patterns to the airport of reality—seem incompatible. Do you feel yourself already taking sides? Are you thinking, *I'd rather my pilot were a theologian than a poet any day*? Or are you the kind who is excited because you know that poetry and parables will present you with a more scenic aerial excursion than any set of propositions, no matter how "true"?

The objective versus the subjective, cognition versus intuition, linear thinking versus the leap of faith and imagination—the two approaches even seem to be represented by different personality types. There are those of us who stand back, coolly analyzing and then organizing information to conform to the patterns we recognize in matter and thought; and there are those of us who feel deeply, getting emotionally involved, acting impulsively, expressing ourselves on the basis of gut feelings or intuition. Modern brainwave detectors have helped us map the human brain—both the intuitive/sensitive right brain and the rational/analytical left brain; we all seem to be dominated by one or the other.

Here is where, as artists, the concrete imagery of metaphor fascinates us because it shows us specifics and idiosyncrasies. If you have ever watched a silkworm spinning a cocoon on the underside of a mulberry leaf, or red blood cells skittering through capillaries under a microscope, you know what I mean.

"Abstract principles have only the most tenuous kind of existence," said Virginia Stem Owens. "They are thoughts, and as such,
only exist while they are consciously present in the mind. There *is*
no thought apart from a thinker." She is convinced that after the
Reformation "religion began to drown in a sea of abstractions and
to starve for images. . . . Out of the very Incarnation itself we
extract with our theological tweezers what we discern as principles."[6] Yet that primary event, the Incarnation, showed us simply,
clearly, accessibly, in a way that could be felt, what would otherwise
blind us—the paradox of God in the flesh.

Robert Farrar Capon said, "To expect that the gospel will all be
propositional truth is nonsense. For example, the beauty of the
parables is not in discovering the propositional truth behind them.
The parables are mysteries aimed at greater mysteries."[7]

As writers, we look at the parables of Jesus, acknowledging
that they *are* the word of God, literally. They speak to us in images
deliberately chosen to be perceived by our imaginations. Jesus
rarely explained them; nor do they need explanation. They speak
to us so immediately, without analysis or interpretation, because
they are meant to be seen and felt. As soon as we begin to dissect
them, they become lifeless and abstract.

I am reminded of an afternoon when my youngest daughter
came home from high school, saying in disgust, "Well, today we
dissected a grasshopper. As if *that's* any way to discover what a
grasshopper is."

We know the truth about grasshoppers not from a scatter of
small body parts under a scalpel on a lab table, but from seeing
them arcing up from the long, hot grass in a summer field. As in
good poetry, the vigorous metaphors of the parables will best be

understood by those with skin to feel and ears to hear and eyes to see them, not critically analyzed but whole and alive and immediate.

John Stott, in his work *God's Book for God's People*, gives a fine example of living metaphor in his exposition of the thirteenth chapter of the gospel of John, where Jesus washed his disciples' feet. Stott says:

> Jesus's actions were a deliberate parable of his mission. John seems clearly to have understood this, for he introduces the incident with these words: "Jesus, knowing . . . that he had come from God and was going to God, rose from supper . . ." (verses 3, 4). That is, knowing these things, he dramatized them in action. Thus Jesus rose from supper, as he had risen from his heavenly throne. He laid aside his garments, as he had laid aside his glory and emptied himself of it. He then girded himself with a towel (the badge of servitude), as in the Incarnation he had taken the form of a servant.
>
> Next, he began to wash the disciples' feet and to wipe them with the towel, as he would go to the cross to secure cleansing from sin. After this he put his garments back on and resumed his place, as he would return to his heavenly glory and sit down at the Father's right hand. By these actions he was dramatizing his whole earthly career. He was teaching them about himself, who he was, where he had come from, and where he was going.[8]

The prophet Ezekiel became a living metaphor too. In the early chapters of his prophecy, we are exposed to some almost

incredible show-and-tell, as God demanded that he lay his body
on the line—a living prophecy against wayward Israel and Judah.
Ezekiel was instructed to take a brick and build around it a model
for the city under siege. Then God told him:

> . . . Lie on your left side, and place the punishment of the house
> of Israel upon it; you shall bear their punishment for the num-
> ber of the days that you lie there. For I assign to you . . . three
> hundred ninety days, equal to the number of the years of their
> punishment. . . . When you have completed these, you shall lie
> down a second time, but on your right side, and bear the punish-
> ment of the house of Judah; forty days I assign you, one day for
> each year. . . . See, I am putting cords on you so that you cannot
> turn from one side to the other until you have completed the
> days of your siege (Ezekiel 4:4–8).
>
> . . . Take a sharp sword; use it as a barber's razor and run it
> over your head and your beard; then take balances for weighing,
> and divide the hair. One third of the hair you shall burn in the
> fire inside the city, when the days of the siege are completed; one
> third you shall take and strike with the sword all around the city;
> and one third you shall scatter to the wind . . . Thus says the Lord
> God: This is Jerusalem. (Ezekiel 5:1, 2, 5 NRSV)

This is like *that*. In fact, in metaphor, "this" *is* "that."
Other prophets were also required to live out their message
from God: Jeremiah, who was ordered to bury his linen shorts (as
the *Good News Bible* puts it) in a hole in the riverbank to show how
Jerusalem would be soiled and ruined; Jeremiah, with his broken
clay jar, his baskets of good and bad figs, and the ox yoke that he
had to fashion from wood and wear around his neck as a symbol of

the slavery of God's people. Then there was Hosea, who was told to deliberately marry a "wife of harlotry" whose marital infidelities spoke clearly of Israel and her worship of idols. Hosea wrote his prophecy out of the acute agony of personal grief, but his persistent love in reclaiming his promiscuous wife was a living metaphor of God's willingness to forgive Israel.

And don't forget Jonah, who was reluctant to do *anything* God told him, but to whom, incredibly, Jesus compared himself, likening Jonah's three days in the fish's belly to his own three days of burial in the ground.

Rib Cage

Jonah, you and I were both signs to unbelievers.
Learning the anatomy
of ships and sea animals the hard way—
from the inside out—you counted (bumping your stubborn head)
the wooden beams and the great curving bones and left
your own heart unexplored. And you were tough.
Twice, damp but undigested, you were vomited. For you it was
     the only way out.
No, you wouldn't die.
Not even burial softened you
and, free of the dark sea prisons, you were still
caged in yourself—trapped
in your own hard continuing rage at me and Nineveh. For
     three nights
and three days dark as night—as dark as yours—
I charted the innards
of the earth. I too swam

in its skeleton, its raw underground. A captive in the belly of
the world
(like the fish, prepared by God)
I felt the slow pulse at the monster's heart, tapped its deep
arteries, wrestled its root sinews,
was bruised by the undersides of all its cold bony stones.
Submerged,
I had to die, I had
to give in to it, I had to go all the way down
before I could be freed to live for you and Nineveh.[9]

Jonah's experience teaches us in living color how God's grace can bring something good out of the most unwilling service.

And Zechariah. God told him: "Act the part of the shepherd of a flock of sheep that are going to be butchered. This will illustrate the way my people have been bought and slain by wicked leaders." The story is complex but fascinating. You may want to read Zechariah 13 for yourself. The prophet concluded the story—"Those who bought and sold sheep were watching me, and *they knew that the* LORD *was speaking to them through my actions*" (Zechariah 11:11 NLT, italics mine). His witness was convincing. He lived his metaphor.

We all—artists, writers, visionaries—find ways to live and explore metaphor in our lives. We look for it: a vivid, four-color picture of what God is saying to us. We find delight in imagery, enjoying it as a literary form, learning more about faith life through scriptural metaphors.

One of my most valued metaphors, one that has captured my imagination again and again from different parts of the Bible—given how much I learn from nature, you won't be surprised—the metaphor of green and growth.

Once, when I was traveling in Israel, I joined a carload of friends driving down to Jericho and Masada. (I say *down* because we dropped fourteen hundred feet as we followed the winding road from the Mount of Olives to Dead Sea level.) It was hot—over 110 degrees at 10:00 a.m.—and Jericho gleamed at us like a green jewel from a setting of sterile sand and glare. Just inside the town limits, we stopped at a roadside booth displaying luscious loquats, figs, oranges, honey, and almonds.

There was a striking contrast between the side of the street on our left that stretched—a dusty wilderness, bare and lifeless—all the way to the glittering Salt Sea, and the Jericho side of the street that was thick with palm trees, orange groves, fig trees, and luxuriant flowering vines. What made the difference? If we stood quiet and listened, we could hear the gurgle of water running through the open, stone-lined irrigation ducts that crisscrossed the city in every direction. Water was the secret of the green.

As we sucked on juicy, sweet loquats, we knew existentially why God used this image of refreshment again and again in the Psalms and Prophets as he described the blessings of his presence. As a poet, this is what I recognize: living metaphor, the images gaining rich life as I recall the words on the pages of Scripture. These are things, we as artists pay attention to, and the medium we find at work in ourselves.

I love the diversity of water sources and of trees in the description in Isaiah 41:18–20:

I will open rivers on the bare heights, and fountains in the midst of the valleys; I will make the wilderness a pool of water, and the dry land springs of water. I will put in the wilderness the cedar, the acacia, the myrtle, and the olive; I will set in the desert the

cypress, the plane and the pine together, so that all may see and
know . . . that the hand of the Lord has . . . created this. (NRSV)

A promise that God wants to bless a multiplicity of people in a
multiplicity of ways. Like a teacher with a diversity of students,
he is saying, *"You're* an acacia, and *you're* a cypress, and *you're* a
pine. You don't have to look like everybody else, and you may
flourish in a different kind of environment than some of your
brothers and sisters in Christ, but you all need water at your
roots." It's the water, often invisibly seeping up from underground, that makes possible the visible growth—the fresh green
of the foliage, the fragrance and color of flowers, the rich sweetness of fruit. All this, as I read, I pay attention to.

In another of Isaiah's brief metaphors, the familiar Eastern
image of a well in a desert oasis is compared with God, the source
of inexhaustible help and blessing, on whom we may draw daily
and be filled with joy, as our thirst for him is satisfied continually.
(Salvation here is not a one-time event but a continuing process.)
The *Good News Bible* puts it this way: "As fresh water brings joy to
the thirsty, so God's people rejoice as he saves them" (12:3), which
makes it a little more prosaic but still a refreshing thought! What is
happening in this metaphor is that some of the meaning attached
to a concrete reality (a well, or a spring of water) is transferred over
to something larger and more abstract and complex and therefore
much more difficult for us to grasp, in this case—*salvation.*

Metaphor makes it real to us, manageable, comprehensible. (Of
course, this may also be a drawback because the very specificity of
the metaphor can narrow its impact. Salvation is like a lot of things
other than a well of fresh water, and this particular focus is only one
of a number of possible images.) Metaphor is imagination *serving*

truth. As we are seeing, God consistently uses this imaginative way of helping us to translate what we may think of as abstract "spiritual truth" into something accessible and possible, and *real*.

Begin with me to look, as artists, at this ongoing service that metaphor offers truth. We see it richly in Scripture, and we begin to understand that this becomes for us, too, the mode with which we speak and paint and write and dance, for these pictures serve the possible, the *real*. It is, indeed, our starting place.

Look, too, in the New Testament. We know Jesus to be an unparalleled storyteller (countless artists and writers have learned the power and value of story through him). He used a story, a parable, an image to point to something we can see with our physical eyes, and then joined it to something else—the spiritually perceived reality. Many of Jesus's images are brief declarations like these: "You are the salt of the earth"; "You are the light of the world"; "I am the bread of life" (Matthew 5:13–14; John 6:35 NRSV).

Other images/metaphors of Jesus are more complex—the seed flung across the soil by the sower is likened to the words of God that fall and take root in listeners' hearts with varying degrees of success. The wise man who constructed his house on a rock foundation and the short-sighted man who built on sand show us clearly and vividly the value of the eternal foundations that underlie our lives.

Most of the time Jesus didn't explain his stories—the parables. In only two instances, after telling the parable of the sower and seed, and the parable of the wheat and the tares, when his disciples came *asking* him for an explanation, did he give a clue as to what they were about. The parables are all built around metaphors—the farmer building bigger barns, or someone finding a lost coin, stray sheep, or precious pearl. For don't we as readers, as artists, as those who look at form and message, believe this: that Jesus wanted his hearers to *feel* the link between the story he was telling and their own personal lives?

A kaleidoscope of biblical metaphors illuminates, Christ and *his* work and worth to us: He's the bread freshly baked and broken. He's the kernel of wheat that decays in the ground in order to sprout and produce more grain. He's the wine poured out. He's the cornerstone of the building. He's the door to a sheepfold—the place of safety and rest. In the same setting the action changes, and he is now the Shepherd who names and loves each sheep individually and leads them out to pasture as well as rescuing them from clinging brambles and mountain cliffs. He's the powerful, untamed, golden-maned lion of royalty. By contrast, he is also the simplicity of a white-fleeced lamb, innocent, helpless, submissive, and sacrificial.

Jesus is seen through a score of vivid images that flood us with a sense of his diversity and infinity and uniqueness. And perhaps the ultimate metaphor for Christ is the Incarnation—the Logos made flesh, narrowed down to the span of a small-town carpenter, so that we could see what God looks like.

Each image is timeless, contemporary, concrete, creative. For artists, for writers of faith, this is the place we learn metaphor as spiritually important and instilled within a framework of image and story.

Often young writers tend to sentimentalize and generalize. But rather than speaking in abstracts or talking in large, nebulous generalities, good writing needs to be—as we have seen it flooding the

teachings of Scripture—tied to concrete images and details, what
C. S. Lewis called "the tether and pang of the particular."[10] It's
important to paint a picture, as Jesus did, that the reader can see or
feel his or her way into. An abstraction can't do that. When young
writers write about love or anger or some other primal emotion, it
often begins as a blurry cloud without any real shape or color. But
when they learn to write about a specific relationship or experience
in three-dimensional detail, we begin to see a picture.

Here's where metaphor comes in. A metaphor carries meaning
over from one arena of life to another. I was excited, when in
Greece, to realize that *metaphoros* is the modern Greek word for
"moving van." Walter Wangerin has said: "Metaphor is two stones
set down beside each other with no explanation." The very fact that
the two stones are there together compels us to make comparisons,
to notice similarities or differences. A metaphor doesn't explain but
illustrates something true by showing us something else that illustrates the same truth.

An illustration or symbol is a likeness to reality. It is *like* and
also *unlike*. *Real* enough in itself, it points the way to a more
meaningful reality. The familiar symbols of bread and wine in
Holy Communion, for instance, speak to us of Jesus's body and
blood. Bread and wine are physically real and almost universally
recognizable as the archetypal food and drink. While they are
like Jesus's body and blood (in color, in texture, in form—solid
and fluid), they are also unlike it. Bread and wine are common,
but Christ's body and blood are unique, broken and poured out
"once for all" (Romans 6:10 NRSV) (though celebrated whenever
we participate in Eucharist). Our imagination transfers the stark
visual images of the physical cells and tissue of body and blood
to another level, on which we perceive the meaning of the sym-

bols: Jesus, broken and made available for our spiritual life and
nourishment.

> *As at his dark birth and death*
> *we had his body in our fingers,*
> *now, again, we split the whiteness*
> *of his loaf by turns, and tasting*
> *his imaged life against*
> *the cup's cool rim*
> *we take him in.*[11]

Thus, in the sacramental pattern of life, everything *means*
something, everything may be a pointer to the holy. The connections, the comparisons, the metaphors, the sounds are all there,
waiting to be recognized. The dazzling of truth may be gradual,
but it is inevitable for those with eyes open to see.

As a poet who values metaphor for all the meaning therein, it
seems increasingly clear that metaphor pervades both our material and nonmaterial worlds. Like a signature, this mark from
God's mind is imprinted in every created entity—a pattern of relationships and likenesses that acts to integrate and fuse the disparate elements of the universe. Think of the words *concrete* and
discrete that speak of observable realities that either cohere or dis-
integrate. From the beginning the presence of these metaphorical
connections persists in Scripture and common life, allowing us to
create art that has transcendent value.

Chapter Four

Learning from Story

I love to tell the story
of unseen things above.
Of Jesus and his glory,
of Jesus and his love . . .

This Sunday school song that echoes from my earliest memories suggests a question: Just how do we tell the story of *the unseen?* So, it's about Jesus and his glory. But how and when have we witnessed heavenly glory? We can perhaps speak of Jesus's love with great personal authenticity, but without viewing Jesus in the flesh, words fail us again. Without the visuals, how do we know enough to form a narrative? Is imagination useful here, or may it lead us into dangerous waters?

Narrative is a word originally derived from the Latin *noscere*, "to know," and a related word *gnarus*, "knowing." Perhaps that is another way of saying that story is how we come to know the world. We live in a world susceptible to narrative. We all find ourselves, without ever asking for it, to be part of a cosmic story that continually unfolds as future becomes present becomes past. I sometimes think of our lives as open-ended novels, with our calendars, journals, correspondence, photo albums, computer files, and our grown children and grandchildren marking the work-in-progress as the plot develops and the characters evolve. Who knows what change-points of circumstance or relationship will transform us in the next weeks or months or years?

We try, in the moment, to make sense out of what may often seem horrifying, incongruous, paradoxical, irrelevant, and absurd, while retaining a kind of eschatological hope that God's order, peace, design, and glory will fill all the spaces in our widely scattered personal and cosmic jigsaw puzzles. We look forward to a time when, like Moses, after his Sinai encounter with Yahweh, our faces will shine in a way that no earthly story could illuminate.

Meanwhile, here we are, caught in time and rooted in space. Time, multiple and fluid as it is, is an essential part of story. And as we might guess, the word *story* is linked with the word *history* (from the Greek word *historia*, "the learning that comes by narrative telling"). Without a sense of time, the forward movement of living and growing, of purpose and events and progress and change, the shape of history and living would be without meaning. As a Christian, I believe that life has meaning, that we are heading somewhere. And as an artist, a poet, I believe in giving voice and picture—record—to that meaning.

The story of the world is imprinted everywhere—the growth rings of trees, the wind- and water-carved art of coastal sandstone rocks, sharp "young" mountains like the Tetons contrasted with the older range formations of the Himalayas and the Andes, the upended strata of geological shift, inscribed parchments and tablets, the artifacts discovered in archaeological digs, the fossil evidence, and the eroding edges of continents that cannot be reclaimed any more than lost innocence.

Story has the power to grasp bits of the past and carry them into the imaginative present, rescuing us from the pitfalls of abstraction. It is not insignificant that much of the Bible, including the deuterocanonical books, is narrative in form and that the characters and plots revealed on the sacred pages are not so different from those that surround and involve us today.

As Eugene Peterson says:

Story is the primary way in which the revelation of God is given to us. The Holy Spirit's literary genre of choice is story. . . . The biblical story comprises other literary forms, sermons and genealogies, prayers and letters, poems and proverbs, but *story* carries them all in its capacious and organically intricate plot.

Further, Peterson says:

Somewhere along the way, most of us pick up bad habits of extracting from the Bible what we pretentiously call "spiritual principles" or "moral guidelines," or "theological truths" and then corseting ourselves in them in order to force a godly shape on our lives. . . . Mighty uncomfortable. . . . [But] it's not the gospel way. *Story* is the gospel way.

Story isn't imposed on our lives; it invites us into its life. As we enter and imaginatively participate, we find ourselves in a more spacious, freer, and more coherent world. We didn't know all this was going on! We had never noticed all this significance! . . . Story brings us into more reality, not less, expands horizons, sharpens both sight and insight. Story is the primary means we have for learning what the world is, and what it means to be a human being in it. No wonder that from the time we acquire the rudiments of language, we demand stories.[1]

Story is perhaps the most familiar and accessible way for human beings to understand the world. Every time we tell a story or write a poem or compose an essay, we give chaos a way of reintegrating into order; we reverse entropy; pattern and meaning begin to overcome randomness and decay. We find satisfaction in juxtaposition and linkage and succession and resolution as things split and differentiate and flow together again.

Not that it is all prepackaged and programmed. Freshness and new insights happen in a continuous stream as we learn from our own stories, and beyond. How many of us writers—novelists, poets—are taught by the words and images that come to us (like unexpected gifts, without our even trying) from quite literally, God knows where?

The short story writer Dorothy Canfield talked of

a generally intensified emotional sensibility. . . . Everybody knows such occasional hours or days of freshened emotional responses when events that usually pass almost unnoticed, suddenly move you deeply. . . . I have no idea whence this tide comes . . . but when it begins to rise in my heart I know that a story is hovering in the offing.[2]

In the gospel of Matthew, chapter 13, Jesus's friends ask him, "Why do you tell stories?" It's a good question. Often a gospel parable will start out with the words, "The kingdom of God is like—" and then proceeds to sketch a story that may be hard for us to comprehend in terms of that kingdom. We often wonder why some of the Jesus stories seem to complicate or even obscure rather than clarify and simplify truth. Perhaps it's that God, who knows us better than we know ourselves, is not content to speak simply to the rational intelligence, but he informs us instead through imagination, intuition, wonder, and epiphany in moments of crystal insight and lifetimes of pondering.

The parables were not merely meant to be dissected analytically; they were designed to be absorbed by the senses and the imagination and *felt*, the subtext of ideal, principle, and truth absorbed almost unconsciously as the mental image and the quickening power of narrative suffuse the understanding over a period of time, a kind of divine soft-sell salesmanship. And this, in our time, is the Spirit's work.

As artists, we move toward the complex, as those who seek to imitate the open door to the heart and to the imagination that Jesus offered through story. To be satisfied with a simplistic approach, then, or a sentimental one, will never seem right, in light of the Gospels.

We, like those followers of Jesus, have glimpses of knowing, of seeing something transcendent that confirms our faith. But because it is *faith*—having to do with things not yet seen—we also must often live with (and as artists, explore) the biblical experience of feeling baffled and puzzled and even skeptical.

The greatest mystery of all was the Incarnation—eternal Spirit, mighty God becoming flesh in Jesus Christ. Like Mary we ask, "How can this be?" And as we try to penetrate the mystery, we are compelled to enter narrative mode. The disjunction brought about by the Fall, the rupture in divine-human relations, compels us to ask the narrative queries: Who? What? When? Why? How?

The *when* is a complex matter of history and archaeology. The *why* invites us into the arena of the Almighty's ongoing desire to bring humanity back into unity and harmony with himself, through what Peterson calls "passionate patience" as the Creator subjects himself to our human temporality. The *what* is an ongoing revelation of the divine. The *how* is quite beyond us—the visitation of the angel, the pregnancy of a virgin, the singing angels, and the traveling star. But the *who* was God bringing within our human vision a form of himself that human beings like John *could* see and hear and touch. "From the very first day we were there, taking it all in—we heard it with our own ears, saw it with our own eyes, verified it with our own hands. The Word of Life appeared right before our eyes; we saw it happen!" (1 John 1:1–2 MSG)

That's the kind of epiphany we explore in our writing, our painting. Sometimes it comes to us like a gift, out of the blue, and all we can say is "Thank you. Thank you."

My senses are the five wide-open windows of my soul. Does this sound too "poetic," too self-consciously sentimental to be real? The sort of popular emotion one might expect to encounter in a Hallmark greeting card?

It is, nevertheless, a rational observation verified by my imagination. My senses—sight, smell, touch, hearing, taste—welcome the arrows of morning sunlight (and with that light comes not only sight but insight, in-*sight*!) into the room of fairly drab, functional furniture that is my logical mind. The sensuous connections flow naturally.

Every day, when I watch the green ferns and Oregon grapes growing behind my house and finger the velvet moss in the verdant ravine under my study window, I think *growing*. When I breathe into my lungs the spiced sharpness of morning mist moving across our Pacific Northwest lake, I am reminded of *the air of prayer*. When I look up at looming, capped-with-snow Mount Baker, with its signature wisp of vapor, I wonder, *Is this a metaphor for God-strength, God-presence?* The thundering rattle of breakers on the pebbled shore of Puget Sound enters my ears like an echo of what God's voice might sound like. The surging tides pushing in and out of Bellingham Bay suggest to me the push and pull of my own story of faith and of creativity.

And I strive within my writing, my story, to pay attention not only to the facts but also to the sensory details and the interior work. Jesus blessed those with "ears to hear and eyes to see," again and again appealing to these human sense organs, and the "eyes and ears of the heart" that lie even deeper in the seeker, to penetrate the thicket of meaning in the gospel stories.

So, why tell stories? To create readiness, to nudge people toward receptive insight. Have you noticed that even in the Sunday sermon, as soon as the preacher uses an anecdote to illustrate his theme, our ears prick up? We all love to hear stories.

The more we see and accept divine revelation, the more we will be shown on earth and the better we will be prepared for the brilliance of heaven. Persistent *rejection* of or indifference to the messages carried by God-story and metaphor will, conversely, so atrophy our inner optic nerves and block our souls' auditory canals that true perception becomes impossible. But for the open-eyed, the stories of Jesus speak vividly.

I am fascinated to realize, along with the painter Marc Chagall, that "any moral crisis is a crisis of color, texture, blood, and the elements of speech, vibration, et cetera—the materials with which we are, like life, constructed."

When we see that narrative, including a moral crisis, is indeed made up of the physical elements—the material from which we are constructed—as we write or paint or dance or sing using those materials of life, we constantly hearken to the Bible's model, which we see in the heart of our own creative process.

The Bible doesn't teach theology systematically. It tells stories. It chronicles human failures and triumphs, it voices human lament and celebration. God reveals himself through the stories and poetries developed by the human authors who wrote the books of the Bible.

So, as a writer, an artist, as one who reads the scriptural stories of faith, one who learns through sensual detail and the Spirit's interior work, I believe that my learning faith and writing about it are gifts from God and that they have value; therefore I persist in telling stories, in chronicling human failures and triumphs—"the crisis of color, texture . . . speech."

Chapter Five

Celebrating Imagination

It has been said that faith is "a certain widening of the imagination." When at the angel's announcement that she would conceive and bear a son, Mary asked the angel, "How shall these things be?" she was asking God to widen her imagination.

All my life I have been requesting the same thing—"a baptized imagination" as C. S. Lewis called it, with a wide enough faith to see the numinous in the ordinary. Without discarding reason or critical analysis, I seek from my muse, the Holy Spirit, images that will open up reality and pull me in to its center.

I have found that as I allow the created universe and the ingrained Scripture to illuminate me, what I deeply believe pushes up through the fabric of words, often in the most surprising and unplanned way. Usually my compulsion to write comes simply from my astonishment at a striking image. (Poetry is, after all, "the language in which we explore our own amazement," as poet Christopher Fry put it.) But again and again the result suggests how the partnership of art and spirituality probes the meanings that lie beneath the surface of all phenomena, waiting to be recognized and acknowledged.

Imagination, which is spirituality's other half, is the window to the soul/spirit. Several years ago I heard Stuart Briscoe use a striking illustration in a conference address. He told of a young man who felt intimidated by the idea of reading the Old Testament. To his mind it seemed like a huge, old, dark, decrepit, dusty house that he was fearful to enter until someone showed him that it was shot through with the rays of joy that were like sunbeams shining through its leaded window panes.

That picture, that way of inviting the imagination, has stayed with me. Morning by morning at home I read my Bible sitting next to an east window. On the sill stands a collection of antique, cut glass bottle stoppers, and at dawn in winter as the sun rises and shines through those multiple small prisms, the room is transformed with rainbow fragments glancing all over the walls and ceiling, filling the room not only with light but with iridescent color. In the old house of Stuart's story, I can visualize the beveled edges of those leaded glass windows turning clear sunlight into rainbows.

Words are like those window prisms, and the rooms of the Bible are lit up, not just with joy but with the magic of metaphors, imagery, story, and pictures in color projected on floors, walls, and ceilings through windows built into the old house by the master architect.

If words are the prism, your imagination is the eye that recognizes *in metaphor,* the colors of the spectrum of experience and their relationship to the source of light—the truth from God.

We need more poets, artists, musicians, and intuitive thinkers who will call us all to recognize, develop, and properly exercise the imagination.

You notice that I qualified that last statement—"properly." How do we *properly* exercise the imagination? Many Christians look at the whole idea of imagination with suspicion and fear. It is too subjective, they feel; it leads us into emotionally based decisions and attitudes. Poets and artists are pretty unstable anyway—let's face it; all that counterculture business and free love and liberation theology and radical politics and living in those unhealthy garret studios or communes with no steady job to bring in the money— idealistic, quaint, but irresponsible! How much safer it seems to trust our lives to establishment and expectations, and to follow tried-and-true formulas and espouse middle-class values and the security of rules and regulations. Imagination? Metaphor? Art? It's dangerous.

In support of that view, which large segments of the church have espoused for centuries, verses like Genesis 6:5 come to mind: "God saw that the wickedness of man was great in the earth, and that every imagination of the thoughts of his heart was only evil continually" (KJV). And in Psalm 2 David asks, "Why do the heathen rage, and the people imagine *a* vain thing?" (KJV). How can God *encourage imagination?*

To be sure, as with all God's good gifts, imagination may be perverted, may be turned by the devil to the kind of rebellious, destructive, idolatrous plotting against God that these verses describe. The ancient Israelites were forbidden the use of "graven images" of even the most beautiful objects, for fear of diverting the attention and worship and loyalty of the people away from God. Yet the Lord God continued to speak to and exercise his people's imaginations in other and startling ways. Contrary to prevailing attitudes, thinking with the imagination, with metaphors, is one thoroughly biblical way for us to peer at and recognize and comprehend God's truth.

Imagination is a word that names "our human ability to form and bring into focus mental pictures, or images, of things that may not be, at a given moment, observable by our physical senses." It involves not only the *memory* of real people and events and past scenes but the ability to create or fantasize or *invent* that which has never before had reality; in other words, to originate new realities, at least in our minds. This approaches the kind of imagination employed by God in the creation of the universe. It's the ultimate in "possibility thinking"!

The word *image* from which *imagination* is derived, has about two inches worth of definitions in *Webster's,* but basically it means a reflection or "an imitation of reality" (*imitari* is its Latin root), and it is a distant cousin of the word *symbol,* which means "the same as."

As we saw in the previous chapter, *metaphor* adds the idea of the transfer of meaning from one object over to another, linking the two by analogy, where metaphor says, *"This* is like *that."* A metaphorical image shows a likeness to a reality but also an unlikeness—it is similar, but it is not identical. For example, in the metaphor "the ship plows the sea," we understand the likeness between a ship moving across the ocean, dividing the water and throwing it up into a wake as it moves along, and a plow pushing through the soil and turning it over in a wavelike furrow. But the ship and the plow are made differently and move through different media even though one may be a striking metaphor of the other. Metaphorical language and the metaphorical way of thinking lie at the heart of poetry and of all the creative arts.

Metaphor and imagination go together. They have an ongoing relationship, linked as intimately as lovers. How would we ever grasp the meaning and power of a metaphor without imagination? And how would the human imagination flourish without metaphors and images to feed on?

One of the symptoms of our age is its tunnel vision, by which we fragment the universe. Life is extraordinarily complex. How can we handle more than a few facets of existence at a time? Our inability to do so means that we are confined to doing our own narrow little thing. The politicians are absorbed with lobbying and debate and the perils of vote fraud and campaign contributions and popularity polls. The musicians live in their own world of rehearsals and instruments and arrangements and contacts and bookings and tonalities and practice, practice, practice. Doctors fight to keep up with the newest developments in diagnosis or drug therapy or surgical procedures under the crushing pressures of rounds and office hours. And so it goes—farmers, mechanics, missionaries, teachers, merchants, pastors, scholars. Not even a Buckminster Fuller or an Isaac Asimov or a C. P. Snow can keep up with it or pull it all together.

It is my wild hope that perhaps creative Christians, by means of their "baptized imaginations," may be able to help integrate the universe by widening and sharpening their focus, by seeing the whole picture as if through God's eyes, by observing humankind and the environment and saying, "Yes, I see. This *is* like that. There is meaning in it."

An example of this possibility shows up in the life of Dorothy Sayers. In James Brabazon's biography, he discussed Dorothy's friendship with Charles Williams and commented:

> At the heart of all the contrasts between them was one fundamental difference: that where Dorothy expounded the laws of the spiritual world like an exceptionally brilliant law student, Williams seemed actually to inhabit that world, and to understand in his blood and bones the truths of which the laws were merely man-made formulations. [1]

In a letter, Dorothy said of Williams:

> He was . . . a practicing mystic; from that point of view I am a complete moron, being almost wholly without intuitions of any kind. I can only apprehend intellectually what the mystics grasp directly. . . . I can only enter into Charles' type of mind to some extent, by imagination, and look through its windows, as it were, into places where I cannot myself walk.[2]

And so she learned from him, and so we learn from each other. For me, one of the motivating impulses and the joys of writing poetry is to let others in on the imaginative world I glimpse from time to time.

Jesus reminded us of the importance of having eyes to see and ears to hear (Mark 4:9). His general revelation—the created universe around us with its built-in reflections of his character—is there for our observation. If we listen, we can hear "the heavens telling God's glory and the firmament proclaiming it—day unto day pouring forth speech and night unto night declaring knowledge." If we see, with both our outer and our inner eyes, we will affirm what the apostle Paul claimed in the first chapter of Romans: "Ever since the creation of the world his eternal power and divine nature, invisible though they are, have been understood and seen in the things he has made" (v. 20 NRSV). What a marvelous paradox: the invisible—understood and seen!

While this kind of vision may be present embryonically in many human souls, it is a gift that must be developed, especially if we are to be truly insightful in creative life. *(Insight*—that inner seeing of imagination.) If we are to interpret and communicate life experience correctly, it is vital that we cultivate an active imagination in ourselves and our students that sees through, *beyond,* the flat window glass of dailiness, with its dust and fingerprints and uneven reflections, to the three-dimensional landscape on the outside, with its movement and light and shadow, its color and contour and texture, its nearness and distance, its changes of weather and season. We must see *through* surface experience and phenomena to their true reality and significance. George Herbert wrote:

> *A man may look on glass*
> *on it may stay his eye,*

or, if he pleaseth, through it pass
and then the heaven espy.

Here meaning has been derived from an image, because imagination jumps the gap from the surface reality of the glass to the
suggestion of meaning that lies beyond it, at another intuitively
felt level.

Imagination is like a videotape on which the memory of green
and the sounds of leaves and rushing water are recorded. I play it
again and again, and I can repeatedly recapture my sense of God's
powerful presence by imaginative faith.

Think of the psalmists' richly imaginative and extraordinary
images from nature and their own experience, which remain accessible to us in our century. It's astonishing to me how Scripture does
that; we're not a nation of shepherds, yet we still understand what
a shepherd is and how David's early life was formed. We understand how the psalms came into being because of the lonely life he
lived on the hills, his dealing with predators, both animal and
human, and his habit of putting his feelings about God's presence
or absence into words.

So our imaginations are a vital part of our psyche, a part
planted there by God for a purpose; imagination is something to
be used not just to teach but also to enrich creativity and to bring
enjoyment.

There has been an overreaction in some circles to the idea of
using the imagination through practices like meditation and
proactive prayer, which visualize how something happens. For
me, however, this is an absolutely wonderful way of exercising
faith. If our imaginations are broadened enough, something that
seems unbelievable to us can seem possible; and we can come to

our prayers expectantly. We broaden our prayer life—and our creative life—by possibility thinking, not by negativism and legalism.

In his Introduction to the book *George MacDonald: An Anthology*, Lewis wrote of his first discovery of MacDonald's *Phantastes* and of the celebrated change it made in his life:

> I knew that I had crossed a great frontier. . . . What it actually did to me was to convert, even to baptise . . . my imagination. . . . The quality which had enchanted me in [MacDonald's] imaginative works turned out to be the quality of the real universe, the divine, magical, terrifying and ecstatic reality in which we all live.[3]

For George MacDonald, his chosen writing forms—poetry and fiction—seem appropriate to this crossed frontier. This may be because these forms are more likely to be imaginative or sensual, matters in which story or image intervenes between writer and reader like a lens, opening up for us a window—baptizing the imagination—offering a different way of absorbing information or of perceiving truth and of responding to it with our senses and our feelings as well as with our rational intelligence.

Perhaps as C. S. Lewis explored the writings of George MacDonald, so full in imagination and reminiscent of writing that only comes from the wells of the past, he noticed that in recent times we have lost the ancient unity between the poetic and the prosaic. It was Lewis's conviction (and perhaps MacDonald's belief too) that if we saturate ourselves in richly creative literature—in Scripture with its potent imagery; in fiction with its narrative flow and power; in poetry that joins emotion with idea, image, and music, logic with intuition, and proposition with imaginative truth—that division may be healed and unity restored.

Perhaps this is what this chapter has been looking toward: restoration, returning, as those of faith and in the arts, to the baptized imagination, foundationally initiated for us in the writings of Scripture. Here, not only is imagination helpful to us as observers and *interpreters* of life, it is an essential part of the *creative* act that brings life into focus for us.

Chapter Six

Listening to the Muse

Who is the muse of the Christian poet? Am I wrong in supposing he must be the Holy Spirit—that quiet, powerful, almost shy member of the Trinity imaged throughout Scripture as a dove, as oil, as fire, as wind? The Spirit is an artist who knows the value of the creative act from divine experience; he's the one who will baptize my spirit and my imagination and shape the images that he sends into words that bear his own fingerprints.

Often, I find in keeping a reflective journal that when I am prayerfully open to story, imagination, metaphor, and the richness of words, the fingerprints of the Holy Spirit are there—they precede me and inform me. Some writings that speak to this presence are from journal pages.

JOURNAL: JANUARY 2, 1987

I'm making some progress at last on my new project—the sweater
I promised to knit for my friend Candace. The yarn is a joy to work
with—dark charcoal gray with slate blue and black fibers, and
flecks of red and blue and green. It is heavy—that is, it has heft; it
feels substantial as it inches through my fingers onto the needles.

The pattern is a continental one translated, very badly, from
Italian to English, which makes it ambiguous and confusing. Added
to that, the yarn shop owner made some adjustments for this
particular yarn, which is not the yarn the pattern calls for. The
woman's scribbled writing is too indistinct to read easily. It's incom-
plete as well—she doesn't follow through consistently, leaving me
with a lot of guesswork.

What this all means is that I must be my own designer. The
photo of the sweater helps; what sounds impossible in the printed
instructions becomes clearer when I can see the pictured shape
and the patterned textures, knit without seams, all in one piece.
Nevertheless, I've begun it and ripped it out at least four times,
using different sized needles and numbers of stitches to get the
size and shape right.

I am feeling, in the roughness of the yarn as the garment
grows in my hands, and from the repetitious click of the metal
needles, what it is like, also, to knit a life. How experimental it is;
how the instructions are not always intelligible and often make no
sense until I knit them into reality, doing it over and over until it's
right; how when I first start a pattern I can't discern the effect I'm
working toward, but I follow the general idea anyway and see
what happens and adapt as necessary, and finally something inter-

esting and warm and beautiful takes shape under my fingers. A slow process, stitch added to stitch, row to row, the work picked up and put down at odd moments the way one adds to one's own life by fits and starts.

There will be no other sweater just like this, and though I have a pattern of sorts, my own trial and error and decision and will shape it into my own creation. I don't know yet what it will look like finished. But the effort *feels* worthwhile, satisfying.

I am both knitter and knitted one. I can *see* myself taking shape, all my yarns and fibers looped in rows that hold together and capture within them the tiny pockets of air that insulate and comfort the body—the air is part of the pattern, plained and pearled into the pieces. Knitted stitch by stitch, hour by hour, it will take all of the years of my life to finish. Lord, I hope it looks good when it's done—a seamless garment.

JOURNAL: JANUARY 4, 1988

Saw the following quote from Walter Wangerin in *Christianity Today*: "Faith is work. It is a struggle. You must struggle with all your heart. . . . And on the way, God will ambush you."

A poem by George MacDonald spoke to me gently along the same lines:

> *0 Son of man, to right my lot*
> *Naught but thy presence can avail;*
> *Yet on the road thy wheels are not,*
> *Nor on the sea, thy sail.*
>
> *My fancied ways, why should'st thou heed?*
> *Thou com'st down thine own secret stair—*

Com'st down to answer all my need,
Yea, every bygone prayer.

As I visit my son John here in Pensacola, the sun is shining so seductively that I spread a sleeping bag on his narrow balcony and, in spite of the wintry 45 degrees, I put on my swimsuit and luxuriate like a cat in a sheltered spot. I have felt so washed-out looking, winter-white of skin. But more than a tan, my skin simply welcomes the naked heat of the sun. For two contented hours I have lain in it, knitted, read, dozed, meditated, particularly on the MacDonald poem.

Again, as so often before, I felt the secret thoughts rising in me, trusting them to be God-thoughts making themselves known. Which started me reflecting on the Holy Spirit and how he teaches us all things and guides us into truth, as Jesus promised. I checked 1 Corinthians 2:10–16 in the NIV, about how God reveals things to us—my spirit knows my thoughts; God's Spirit knows God's thoughts. Because I am God's daughter, a bridge, a path, a secret stair has been built from his heart to mine so that by the Spirit, God's thoughts can step into my mind. "This is what we speak, not in words taught us by human wisdom but in words taught by the Spirit. . . . The spiritual person makes judgments about these things" because she has "the mind of Christ" (vv. 13, 15, 16). Even these journal words are a part of the process—this mysterious inner interweaving of observation and reflection and verbalization.

As I read or knit under warm sun, thinking these thoughts as they came, not trying to be "creative," the wind suddenly gusted and I saw a scatter of gold leaves flying down from the maple saplings a few yards away beyond the stream. I have been wanting to take a photo to illustrate my poem ". . . let him hear," about leaves falling from the trees at God's command because they hear him more attentively and obey him more instantly than we do. The image there in front of me was perfect. I brought my camera to the porch, focused, framed, and waited for the wind to blow again and release more leaves for my shutter.

Talk about waiting for the Spirit (wind, breath) to stir! That was my literal task. My skin told me when the breeze was beginning, my ears could hear the tinkle of the wind chimes from the porch below. I took shot after shot, and only time and Nikon will tell my success or failure. But the lesson of waiting for the Spirit to move, watching, sensing the "now," obeying the breath, catching him at it, was learned whether or not a perfect image printed itself on the film.

I knew experientially my powerlessness to make a creative moment like that happen. A tree can't thrash its branches; it waits for the wind to move them. I can manufacture neither poems nor spiritual power, but my task is to be on the spot, watching, ready when the breeze picks up.

Aren't you astonished at the way the link between the visible and invisible worlds is made? Faith is not linear. It is, indeed, that widening of the imagination, a leap into the transcendent, a taste of the numinous, the ability to see the extraordinary in the ordinary. And our coach for the leap, the glue in the link, is the Spirit of God.

A phenomenal resource, the Spirit. As Christians and artists, we are not just followers, plodding imitators, or self-propelled innovators. We are empowered from within our own God-given imaginations by the first poet, the primal artist, the original composer. Our own creative spirits, made in the image of another, are boosted and blessed and set on fire by our union with God in Christ.

There is a radical nature to both art and faith. Both are epiphanic "manifestations." Both are transformative; we are changed as we enter their gleaming realms. They are full of inexplicable transitions and showings, mysterious both in their origin and mechanism.

Does art impact our spirituality? Does spirituality affect our art? Yes. And yes. The two seem symbiotic, each feeding on and in turn nourishing the other. They work in tandem; it is hard to imagine an artist who is totally unspiritual in the sense of being out of touch with both created and unseen worlds. And it is hard to imagine a person full of Spirit who is not in some way creative, innovative, world disturbing.

That word *Spirit* in the Greek can mean either breath or wind. Wind is something beyond our control. The Holy Spirit moves in ways we cannot predict or program. I believe, too, that this "breath for the bones" is the animating presence of the Holy Spirit.

I find this to be true on a very practical level.

Often, in the process of writing an article or a poem or an essay, I find myself "stuck," confused, or unable to know in which direction the writing should go. That's when I cry "Help!" and ask the Holy Spirit to guide my listening, my thinking, and my creating into channels that will bring me to the heart of truth for the work. I become a servant of the word rather than its controller. And listening obedience, rather than preplanning, becomes my modus operandi.

In listening for the Spirit, spiritual disciplines are helpful, attuning us to the wavelength of the Word of God and the voice of God. But we need to have our antennae out to receive the messages. Silence and solitude leave us undistracted so that the messages can arrive undistorted, clear, and true.

But so many are afraid of silence and of being alone. They wonder, *What if nothing happens? What if God ignores me? Or what if he isn't there?* But, in gradual steps, and given some simple tools, people can begin to experience contemplation for themselves and discover that it is transformative. And this transformation (as well as the waiting) also informs—always—the place where our creative work is done. For artists, this combination of discipline and listening-receiving is a true cornerstone.

To be an artist, to live out the persistence of spiritual hunger and thirst—those seasons of drought and rain in art, in the weather, and in spiritual vitality—or a sense of connection with God the transcendent Almighty, in the context of an overwhelmingly material universe—is a kind of evidence of spirituality's existence and importance.

In C. S. Lewis's words (I return again and again to his writing), "If I find in myself a desire which no experience in this world can satisfy, the most probable explanation is that I was made for another world."[1] Creativity as well as spirituality do not lend themselves to physical analysis, nor are they susceptible to rational proof. But neither can they be denied. And though invisible and intangible, their very evanescence is a challenge that makes us want them more and draws us out in the strenuous effort of question and search.

And spirituality is very like the creative impulse toward art—often fickle and unpredictable. We have an untamable, undomesticated Spirit (whom we tend to trivialize and formalize in order to feel safe), and the artistic and spiritual gifts from his holy hand

are not to be summoned with a flick of the wrist or a pleading
tone of voice.

Listen to the words of Annie Dillard:

It is the fault of infinity to be too small to find. It is a fault of eternity to be crowded out by time. Before our eyes we see an unbro-
ken sheath of colors. We live over a bulk of things. We walk amid
a congeries of colored things which pan before our steps to reveal
more colored things. Above us hurtle more things, which fill the
universe. There is no crack. Where then is the gap through which
eternity streams? Materials wrap us seamlessly; time propels us
ceaselessly. Muffled and bound we pitch forward from one filled
hour to the next, from one filled landscape or house to the next.
No rift between one note of the chorus and the next opens on
infinity. No spear of eternity interposes itself between work and
lunch.

   And this is what we love . . . our lives, our times, our generation, our pursuits. And we are called to forsake these vivid and pal-
pable goods for an idea of which we experience not one trace? Am
I to believe eternity outranks my child's finger?

She goes on:

The idea of eternity is that it bears time in its side like a hole. Let us
rest the material view and consider, just consider, that the weft of
materials admits of a very few, faint, unlikely gaps. People are, after
all, still disappearing, still roping robes on themselves, still braving
the work of prayer, insisting they hear something, even fighting and
still dying for it. The impulse to a spiritual view persists, and the evidence of that view's power among historical forces and among con-

temporary ideas persists, and the claim of reasoning men and women that they know God from experience persists.[2]

This mystery, this spill of clues to an unseen reality, is very much a part of the artist's as well as the mystic's life. I wait in silence by the sea or in the woods or in the silence of 2:00 a.m. when I cannot sleep, or more likely, in the press of a desk overburdened with other people's urgencies, for a poem to call me, claim me, write *me*, much as I wait, in prayer, for the Spirit to speak, to respond, to direct or correct me. I cannot turn on the writing art or transcendence like a faucet. My job is to wait and see—literally to *wait* for the Spirit, with the Spirit, and to *see*.

In this waiting time I must be sure that my antennae are out, combing the air, ready to pull in the messages. Receptivity, yes. Waiting, yes. Awareness, yes. Active readiness, yes. For passivity has no place in the life of art or of Christian spirituality. Art and belief are not conveniences, nor do they call to us at convenient times. A poem will begin in my head as I prepare a dinner for eight, at which point I am likely to turn absentminded, to break an egg into the garbage disposal or put a pot of hot coffee in the refrigerator and then search for it fruitlessly. God's Spirit will call me to prayer or contemplation or to creating a line of a poem as I am paying my bills or shopping for green beans and avocados. Or my mind will seize one idea after another all night long (when I really *need* the sleep), and I'm grateful for the collection jar of my computer monitor glowing in the dark that catches and holds those unanticipated, uninvited lightning bugs of ideas or phrases for the morning. And when that morning comes, I am so energized by all this electric activity that I don't feel the lack of sleep. Like Dorothy Sayers at the completion of one of her novels, "I feel like God on the Seventh Day!"[3]

While I was a student at Wheaton College, studying English literature under Clyde Kilby, the remarkable teacher who later became my mentor and the honorary grandfather to my children, he presented me with a small paperback book titled *The Creative Process,* edited by Brewster Ghiselin. This was a compilation of essays by phenomenally gifted people in a number of diverse disciplines—astronomy, cosmology, molecular biology, musical composition, philosophy, architecture, theology, and of course, fiction and poetry.

What they had all experienced in common, expressed in their letters, lectures, books, or journal entries, was the sense that their seminal ideas, the images and concepts that were foundational to their most important contributions to knowledge, were *given* them from somewhere outside, beyond them. These gifts arrived unannounced—in what has been called the "Eureka! syndrome." As poet Stephen Spender admitted in that very anthology, "My alpha-plus ideas arrived from God-knows-where, quite literally."

C. S. Lewis explained it like this: "With me, the process is much like birdwatching. . . . I see pictures," and "A whole set might join themselves so consistently that there you had a complete story."[4]

Perhaps you're familiar with his account of how the Narnian Chronicles came into being. As Lewis remembered it: "As with the Ransom stories [his space trilogy], the Narnian tales began with *seeing pictures in my head. The Lion, the Witch, and the Wardrobe* all began with a picture of a faun carrying an umbrella and parcels in a snowy wood."[5] Like a dream, this image appeared from nowhere, demanding that Lewis enflesh it in a story. But of course, it didn't come "from nowhere."

The Spirit plays the role of the muse and proves again and again that God is an artist and knows the value of the creative act from experience, beginning with an image.

But how does my art impact my spirituality? I find this happening most authentically in my journal, where art and spirituality form almost a single river. Because I am one person, one organic individual, my life and mind join in one stream of consciousness. I write in my journal whatever is going on internally at a given moment—the seed of a poem, its early stages of growth, a prayer for help, a suddenly perceived connection, even a joke or a bumper sticker that I want to remember. It is not all "spiritual." It is not all "art." But it is all a part of my life that works to enlarge me on both fronts.

The Muse moves mysterious as ghost.

Ghostly

I think often about the invisible
God—doubly covert. I mean, now and again
Father and Son made their appearances,
speaking bold in thunder, blood,
or salvation. But the Third
Person is a ghost. Sometimes
he silvers for a moment, a moon sliver
between moving leaves. We aren't sure.

What to make of this . . . how
to see breath? As energy

hovering, birdlike, over chaos,
breeding it into ferns and whales;
blessing the scalps of the righteous
with a pungency of oil; bleeding the hard
edge of warning into all those
prophet voices; etching
Ezekiel's view with oddities—
eyes in wheels spinning like astrolabes;
crowding Mary's womb
to seed its dark clay; wising up fools
to improbable truth; filling us like
wine bottles; bursting from our mouths in
champagne gasps of surprise? This for sure—
he finds enough masks to keep us guessing:
Is it really you? Is this you also?

It's a cracked, crossover world, waiting
for bridges. He escapes our categories,
choosing his own free forms—fire, dove,
wind, water, oil—closing the breach
in figures that flicker within
the closed eye, tongue the brain, sting
and tutor the soul. Once incarnate
in Judaea, now he is present (in us
in the present tense), occupying our bodies—
shapes to be reshaped—houses
for this holy ghost. In our special
flesh he thrives into something
too frequent to deny, too real to see.[6]

I was driving along a country road when an idea for this poem arrived. Winter was coming; leaves were dying; the landscape was brown, dead; the birds were flying south.

I saw a flock of starlings flying across the sky in a very strong wind, wheeling in its gusts. I began to think of how the physical wind affects the sky and landscape and the parallel between that and how God works by the wind of his Spirit.

God adds the work of the Spirit to the natural universe and brings it to life. We are profoundly affected by the work of the Spirit whether we recognize it or not.

As a writer, one thing that intrigues me is that the level of my Muse's work is invisible. Jesus's words in John 3, describing how the Spirit's work is like the wind, read like this: "You don't know where it's coming from or where it is going" (author's paraphrase).

Often, my poems feel like a gift. In George Bernard Shaw's play, *Joan of Arc,* Joan's captors respond to her claim that she hears God by telling her that it's just "something in her imagination." She responds, "Exactly. That is how God speaks to me, through my imagination." This is very often how I feel—that words, ideas, and rhythms are given to my imagination, handed to me as a gift for which I am infinitely grateful. But the gift must be shaped and crafted if I am to be a cocreator with God.

May Sarton's *Mrs. Stevens Hears the Mermaids Singing,* a novel about a poet and her muses, says some remarkable things about the reasons for poetry—that its catalyst is intense personal relationships.

One of her statements rings in me like a gong: "Loneliness is the poverty of self; solitude is the richness of self."[7] For the mystics, the desert fathers and mothers, solitude was also the richness of the Spirit within and the presence of God. As I think about my own poetry, my heart-cry is that my muse be the mind of Christ within me, that my poetry's catalyst may be an intense, sustained interaction with my Maker.

A story from the life of the poet Denise Levertov is worth recounting here. I quote from her essay "A Life That Enfaiths" in *New and Selected Essays*:

> As I became, a few years ago, more and more occupied with questions of belief, I began to embark on what I'll call "do-it-yourself theology." Sometimes I was merely trying to clarify my mind and note down my conclusions-in-process by means of the totally undistinguished prose of journal entries. Sometimes, however, *it was in poems that the process took place*, and most notably in the first such poem I wrote, a longish piece called *Mass for the Day of St. Thomas Didymus*. . . . The poem began as an experiment in structure.[8]

She thought to herself that it might be possible to adapt the framework of a choral piece that included parts of masses from many periods—medieval, Renaissance, baroque, classical, and modern, not in chronological order, yet with a striking unity because of its liturgical framework. She wrote:

> I thought of my poem as "an agnostic Mass," basing each part on what seemed its primal character: the Kyrie a cry for mercy, the Gloria a praise-song, the Credo an individual assertion, and so on: each a personal, secular meditation. But a few months later, when

I had arrived at the Agnus Dei, I discovered myself to be in a different relationship to the material and to the liturgical form from that in which I had begun. The experience of writing the poem—that long swim through waters of unknown depth—had been a conversion process.[9]

In effect, Levertov had been transformed by her own writing as she experienced unintended changes in her understanding through the poem she was working on and the efficacy of truth and its substance in her unconscious.

We are all, whether we are conscious of it, swimming in waters of unknown depth. St. Paul prayed for his friends that "the eyes of their hearts might be enlightened" (Ephesians 1:18, author's paraphrase). The story is there to be attended to, to be absorbed if we are willing to give it our attention, to follow the path of exploration and observation, eyes and ears alert, to follow the word, even giving over our conscious control of where it will lead. Madeleine L'Engle called this way of life "becoming the servant of the word."

Like Mary, with her available womb; like the ancient prophets, standing in the gap, a foot in two worlds with souls attuned to both heaven and earth; like the psalmists listening for celestial tunes and translating them into the real poetry of both desolation and exaltation; like the Son of God becoming flesh; we fulfill our destinies by telling and retelling the story that weaves together divine transcendence and earthy human experience. And we go forth together, rejoicing in the power of the Spirit.

Part Two

The Details of Creativity:
Exploring the Creative Process

Chapter Seven

Beginning with Journal Writing

JOURNAL: JANUARY 1987

After eight transatlantic hours, the plane lights inside have been dimmed; the light in the sky is fading. Through the plane window, high over the Mediterranean, I can see the orange glow along the horizon melting beneath turquoise, blue, and navy. Though the orange is a hot color, the effect is icy because of the clarity of the air and the frost that creeps up the oblong Plexiglas windows. It's almost an astronaut's view. Is this the way God sees our world, and us?

I'm in the air over Greece now. An illuminated map, green for land, blue for water, fills the screen in the front of the cabin. A red

line traces our plane's progress, inching along as the hours pass.
Somehow, the map seems more real than the land masses out of
sight in the dark below, which have lost actuality for me. Watching
the red line, I have become a part of the map, absorbed in it, separated from the blank darkness the other side of the plane's metal
skin. The lighted display tells us we are going 627 miles an hour at
a height of thirty-six thousand feet. Seeing it makes me wish for an
illuminated map of my own spiritual journey. I want to see clearly
the country I have come from, and what lies ahead, and how fast
and direct is my journey toward it.

Diamonds That Leap

When the leaf fell and brushed my hand
I began to reverse the world. I asked:
What if this warped willow leaf, yellow,

scaled with age, could smooth
to a green blade, then flicker into
the knot of a spring twig, like

a grass snake's tail disappearing, slick
and chill, into his home? That one question—
it was a whirlpool, pulling in

others: What about a river?
Might its waters rush up these indigo
hills of Shenandoah and split to a scatter

of diamonds that leap to their rain
clouds, homing? Can a love
shrink back and back to like,

then to the crack of a small, investigative
smile? Could God ever suck away creation
into his mouth, like a word regretted,
and start us over?

Or this, can anyone enter the mother's womb
and be born, again?[1]

Luci Shaw, *The Green Earth*

As a writer, as a keeper of a daily reflective journal, I find that as soon as I put words and ideas onto paper in my notebook, or type them into my computer, they begin to gather to themselves more images, more words and ideas. As I write I have the sensation of being at the center of a small vortex of enlarging connections, as in the poem above, and my pen or my fingers on the keyboard move faster and faster to keep pace with them.

This growing cluster of words and images reflects not an externally imposed outline, or system, or a preconceived plan, but a more organic development, a kind of evolution from a very small beginning—a leaf, a seed idea, a phrase, a vivid image. Words, ideas, images, all of which have enormous imaginative and emotive power, seem to gain a life of their own—tapping into a great Source that lies beneath them, fleshing themselves out and making a way for themselves as they stretch and expand, with our minds and writing instruments following, becoming

merely a kind of substrate to record them and shape them as
they develop.

Cogitation (which means "together shaking"—the mental dance
of thought with imagination, a cerebral *pas de deux*) accompanies
any art, such as musical composition or dance or painting, rather
than preceding it. What does this mean, in practical terms, for any
artist involved in creative work? For me, it means that I *follow* ideas
and images. If an image shows up, often uninvited, unexpected, I
am called to stop everything and pay attention. And the word *pay*
is significant. There's a cost to it, in time, in energy. But the rewards
are immense.

I tend to write poetry from enthusiasm rather than discipline;
that is, I don't sit down at a set time every day and tell myself, "I
really should write a sonnet." Rather, the iambic beat of a sonnet
will come to me in the night in a specific phrase that calls out,
"Write me!" And I obey. Or a comparison or contrast occurs to
me in my reading or during the Sunday sermon or as I write my
journal, which is where most of my seed poems are recorded.

My writing grows at its own pace, in its own form. I suspect the
same command impels the work of artists in other spheres. Often
it feels like a willful puppy pulling on a leash, leading me in a
direction I hadn't thought of. And I am compelled to follow it,
often with surprising results.

When the Spirit is actively moving me into creativity, I find
myself drawing the writing out of myself much as a spider
draws silk from her own abdomen to fashion her delicate, intricate web. This process is so integral to my thinking and living. I
often say that if I should lose my current journal, filled with
intensely personal responses and events and emotions and ideas,
I would feel that I had lost a part of myself. My *self.*

In journal writing, creativity isn't always carefully planned and programmed. Sometimes it's just a matter of slowing down and giving the mind and soul time to be reflective and responsive, and then listening. And going with what you hear.

The writing, the music, the painting, the art will begin to open doors as it advances, without my always knowing where it is going or what the end result will be. The rational, planning mind does not leap ahead of the intuitive, imaginative mind. They work in tandem, dancing, quivering together. Only then can the surprises that bring the work to life begin to show up. Inevitability and surprise.

Henri Nouwen, in his *Reflections on Theological Education,* wrote:

> Most students . . . think that writing means writing down ideas, insights, visions. They feel that they must first have something to say before they can put it down on paper. For them writing is little more than recording a pre-existent thought.
>
> But with this approach true writing is impossible. *Writing is a process in which we discover what lives in us. The writing itself reveals what is alive . . .* [italics mine]. The deepest satisfaction of writing is precisely that it opens up new spaces within us of which we were not aware before we started to write. To write is to embark on a journey whose final destination we do not know. Thus, creative writing requires a real act of trust. We have to say to ourselves, "I do not yet know what I carry in my heart, but I trust that it will emerge as I write." Writing is like giving away the few loaves and fishes one has, trusting that they will multiply in the giving. Once we dare to "give away" on paper the few thoughts that come to us, we start discovering how much is hidden underneath . . . and gradually come in touch with our own riches.[2]

William Saroyan, an American writer, said: "The task of the writer is to create a rich, immediate, usable past."

A journal offers a way of entering into the process of personal reflection; discovering insight; and growing in maturity, self-understanding, and God-awareness. I feel that keeping a consistent, personal journal is a form of prayer; as I write, honest and transparent to God and myself, I may become conscious of the divine presence directing my thoughts and conclusions. I sense that God is with me in the intimacy gained on these private pages. I can deal with emotional difficulties as I write from the inside out. I can also grow artistically and spiritually as my secret thoughts find their most compelling and honest avenues of expression.

And to those hesitant to start a journal because they are intimidated by the blank pages, or who think they have nothing profound or valid or interesting to say: be brave with words. Here's why: They can free us, nudging us into the kind of confidence in the process that eases our way into writing as a way of discovering and articulating who we are before God. Journal writing urges us to trust God and our own hearts, and such trusting results in fresh and surprising insights that bring great personal enrichment to us and through us to those whom our lives touch.

Not only are journals a place of honest reflection, they are a place for early creative process or where projects begin. We do creative brainstorming in a journal to record what we are seeing in our minds, to learn to focus on the insight of the imagination, to learn to express it, and then to look back at what we have said and pull out certain strands and consolidate and reshape.

It's a process very much like birthing a child. Poems and other art forms have a gestation period. You may have an idea, but it may need to hibernate for years before it's ready to have a life of its own. I tell writers to catch and record these seminal ideas, these seeds, the minute they arrive, or they will be blown away in the wind of active living.

Journal writing is central to helping us see how we've grown, where we've come from, if we have learned from our mistakes and successes, or if we see ourselves repeating the same cycle of futility—of not moving on, not processing things. We can discover a great deal by reading back in our journals.

I've compared rereading a journal to being in a helicopter. When you're walking through a forest on foot in the underbrush, you can't see the lay of the land. You can't see where you are going or if you've changed direction. But if you're in a helicopter, you can view the whole landscape, the tracks through it, the mountains and rivers as well as the contour of the whole terrain.

Even though it can be like plowing rocky ground, in my journal I can keep track of where I am and where I have been. It may not be immortal poetry or even very good prose; it may not say anything very significant, but it's keeping the continuity of my ongoing life.

And when you can't write? When nothing comes? Those unproductive seasons are times for storing. I replenish by reading, reading, reading. You have to allow ideas to fill your reservoir before they're ready to spill over. A writer has to reflect the totality of life, not just the high points.

If I am in pain, feeling lonely or depressed or just downright miserable, writing in my journal offers comfort. I write it all down, and somehow it is cathartic. Much of that pain inside me feels

chaotic. I can't analyze it. As I write it down on the page, it is
drawn out of me, and I can see it with better perspective. There
is the pain on the page!

When you begin to keep a journal, you will find yourself better
able to keep track of your experiences, emotions, and responses to
what is going on. For creative thinking, or mining emotions, or
finding seeds of ideas, your journal essentially becomes a resource.
Perhaps the best way to illustrate this is by ending with a journal
entry.

Journal Entry

Sanibel Island. Standing here on the beach, I find myself at the joining of elements—earth, air, water (and the sun adds the fourth—
fire). The distances are tremendous; a whole continent stretches
itself horizontally away behind me, as does the sea in front of me;
the ocean floor plummets from the continental shelf to an invisible
depth at my feet, dark blue and mysterious; and the sky without
clouds—we can look up forever through the light-years of distance.
All these infinites meet and mark me, and dance with each other,
on this very spot. The edges shift in and out a bit with winds and
tides, but these fundamental borders give us a sense of the universe
and the acts of God.

I am amazed at how effortlessly I slip into a beachcomber role.
As I pad along the shore, eyes scanning the millions of shells in
their textured banks, or scattered, embedded in the film of the
pulled-back waves, my mind keeps saying to me, *This is happiness.
This is the state of purest happiness.*

Bright bits of color catch me in the eye—rosy, rubbery seaweed, a pearly jingle shell, a ribbed calico cockle patterned in bright tangerine, a live sea star, a glistening angel wing—underserved gifts of grace winking up at me with the sheen of sun and sea on them, waiting to be fondled with the eye or carried away with me a thousand miles to where they can remind me of these perfect moments. As I bend and lift each one and love it with my touch and glance, I wonder if this was how God bent and lifted me, how he chose me and treasures me, how he wants me with him. I must seem singular and precious to him if he came so far to find me.

Today, with the wind at fifty knots and the rain driving in, the force of the weather is healing, elemental. Huge breakers endlessly crash against the shoreline, throwing up a salt mist, churning the thick layers of shells and making a clinking rustle as the brine sucks down and away through them. I walk the shore with the wind literally pushing me forward, irresistible as the Spirit. Clouds scud close over me at an oblique angle with the sun suddenly breaking through to water the sea's rough silk with milky light. A rim of rain obscures the horizon. All the gulls, terns, plovers, and sanderlings are standing, cowed-looking but brave on the shore, heads away from the gusts, tail feathers ruffled, waiting for the wind to die.

Last night after dinner a brilliant sunset poured between the clouds like melted gold. I ran down to the beach to catch it on film before the fire died. There's a splendid satisfaction in having a record of the weather in its several moods. I can recall it, courtesy of my photos and my journal, and in some future moment the visual impression will call up the other sense impressions—the tang of the spray driven by the singing air, the buffet of wind on cheekbone, the crunch of shells underfoot, the unceasing sounds of the sea.

J. B. Phillips said that the ocean is irresistibly attractive because it reminds us of eternity. I'd put infinite space in there too, as a link between the sea and the eternal state. The endless in-wrinklings of waves is one clue, the unknown depth another. The waves' continuous arrival shows me an ongoing diversity that is never monotonous because an infinite innovation lies behind it. Each arc of water up the beach, each configuration of shells and stones and dunes and grasses is unique, unrepeatable.

In the aftermath of the storm comes its harvest. The waves and their deep turbulence have knocked loose and laid at my feet shells not seen in the earlier, calmer days of this week. Today I have found apple murex, turbans, zebra nerites, distorsios, jewel boxes, tellins, coquinas, spiny oysters, tulips, turnip whelks, moon snails, babies' ears, many of them alive—that is, with their original inhabitants still attached and lively (though in one helmet I found a squatter—a hermit crab that appeared and disappeared again into its little home quick as a blink).

I find I cannot choose shells for others, nor they for me. The oiled and varnished specimens in the gift shops hold no attraction for me. Sometimes, walking the beach, someone will pick up a shell and hand it to me, but by their choosing it they have already made it theirs. To me shells are a parable of personal choice and significance. A volute or a junonia is fascinating in itself—"a folding out of pink and white/a letting in of spiral light"—but the incident of noticing it in its own setting and taking it for my own renders it notable; its selection is part of its history. Mentally I see any treasured shell in its original company—an aggregate of shapes and sizes in melon, chestnut, dappled mauve, butter yellow, dusk, or taupe. We each search out our own best colors, our favorite shapes.

Chapter Eight

Learning to Risk

Always a truth-seeker, a God-hungerer, in my search I have followed a risky and fascinating track over mountains and valleys. The "ups" have been glorious, true epiphanies, showings, glimpses of God's face in which I've known divine presence and help. Prayers answered. Truths demonstrated and received and acted on.

But some of the valleys have been abysses, places of grief and discouragement, disillusionment and despair.

I've had the joys and pressures of working as a writer. I've learned a lot about popular culture from its indifference to my work as a poet. In addition, I've experienced a turbulent inner life—wounds of the spirit, bereavement. Depression. At such times I've been comforted to know that even Jesus suffered doubt, rejection, frustration, fatigue, despair, even abandonment by God his Father.

You may attribute my uneven progress (I sense there *has* been progress) to the instability of the artistic temperament. And you may be right. Perhaps I wouldn't *be* a poet without the highs and the lows. Perhaps the poet's hypersensitivity to despair and delight, pain and pleasure, ugliness and beauty, meaning and absurdity, color my relationship with God. Perhaps I'm a bit like David the psalmist, another poet, another individual with "a heart after God," a yearning spirit, who also had a bumpy journey. In poetry and life David soared and plunged, both.

Where one part of me has always been eager to pin faith down, examine and control it, another part of me is restless, creative, shaking at the reins, wanting to explore all the other possibilities, knowing that even if I achieved it, watertight certainty is like legalism; it jettisons mystery, renders faith unnecessary, tries to grab the control from God's hands and set up a grid of human rules instead. But with the unpredictable movements of the Spirit of God, faith is more like risk, like charting a course through the turbulent waters of Puget Sound, among all the islands and hidden reefs. We can see the islands and steer our craft clear of obvious obstacles, but the underwater rocks and sandbars, appearing and then vanishing with the tides, are mysteries we cannot fathom, places where we must trust the charts and the skipper's experience rather than clear sightings.

The following is a story of my struggle with risk, tides, reefs, and islands, which I think speaks to faith and to challenges, and also speaks to the life of the artist, to those who wish to live in creative challenge, charting a course and not knowing how it might all play out.

My friend Carol and I, both avid sailors, planned to cross and recross Lake Michigan and explore stretches of its rocky shoreline. This was an adventure. It was also a risk.

At that time Carol and I were beginning new voyages in life and faith. We were both single after decades of marriage—I by widowhood, she by divorce. Single, we were learning to navigate in a couples' world, to steer across new bodies of water, to use the means available to find our way—charts, compass, depth sounder, and the feel of the wind on the cheek.

Just the two of us, no extra crew or skipper, would be sailing out of Sister Bay, Wisconsin, on a twenty-eight-foot sailboat. The owners of the charter marina had been wary. Two women? But Carol had owned and sailed boats most of her life. And I was a natural navigator with an iron stomach, immune to seasickness.

From the beginning there were the familiar sounds: the slap of a loose stay against the metal mast, a repeated squeak, regular as breathing, as the boat rose and fell against the rubber bumpers that protected us from scraping the dock. Light angled down through the ports into the cabin and my open eye.

The sailing world is a unique community with its own lingo. As a novice I learned to ask questions: What's this halyard for? Why can't you set a stern anchor? What's a downhaul? Before our trip, the marina made sure we had a thorough checkout, going through our vessel, *Acquittal*, item by item. Life in a new dimension requires new skills, and it takes time to feel at home with them, competent, ready to move ahead.

Early in the morning of our first full day, the water was as smooth as obsidian. So we made our way up the curving coastline of Green Bay with the motor. When a light wind began to ruffle the surface, the water looked like seamless yardage of gray silk, with gulls floating on it like nubs in the fabric. Even the most fearsome bluff of all, Death's Door, site of many shipwrecks, looked deceptively mild and unthreatening in the sun-filled day.

By evening we reached Washington Island and threaded our way between the colored buoys into a perfect little harbor. After supper we went on deck to watch a complex light show—a sunset evolving through orange and pink to purple, with Vs of geese overhead. No noise—no breakers even. Only a remote fog-horn sounding regularly, like a small, systematic ghost.

Tranquility covered us like a sheet. The quietness hummed; it crowded the ears. The boat moved ever so slightly at anchor, as though touched by a child's single finger.

But by 4:30 a.m. we woke to hear the wind singing in the stays after a sudden unexpected thunderstorm. The wind was blowing in just the direction we needed, but we knew how quickly that could change. Out on the open lake, we watched the land behind us evaporate into a thin blue line and disappear, leaving us alone in an infinite circle of water—Lake Michigan. Being out of sight of land is a kind of limbo, of feeling "nowhere." It is a new region whose lack of landmarks mirrored our own single state.

Five-foot waves made *Acquittal* pitch and yaw. To stay on our heading meant constant effort—a tensing of arm on the tiller against the contradictory tug of wind and wave.

We began to get a bit anxious when by 2:00 p.m. we hadn't sighted the Manitou Islands and the sky was darkening ominously in the west. Finally, we thought we saw something. One minute it was there; the next, the horizon seemed empty again. An hour later we were sure—the huge dunes of Sleeping Bear gleamed in faint, golden crescents, lighter than sea and sky. Seeing the shore brought a sense of peace, a comforting certainty.

The next morning was an easy run to Leland, Michigan, on the mainland. We entered Leland early, hoping for a berth, but about thirty boats returning from the Mackinac Race were already jammed into the harbor, colorful pennants flying from all their stays. The only options left were to raft (tie up) to other boats, side by side like sardines, or anchor in the open water of the harbor, which we did.

More of the Mackinac fleet came in, and the wind was strong even inside the breakwater. The situation grew tense. In the small, crowded harbor, we didn't want to swing into other boats in the night if the wind shifted. On the hot, windy afternoon we rowed ashore for supplies. The land was heaving. I could feel myself walking with the rolling gait of an old salt and wished the earth would steady under me.

That night the harbor was stacked even more tightly with boats. Thunderstorms were predicted, and we were worried. What would happen when the wind changed? Would our anchor drag?

At 4:00 a.m. I woke to thunder. Every few seconds the portholes were bright with lightning. Suddenly we heard a panicky voice from nearby: "Hoy, *Acquittal*! Watch out, you guys! You're drifting down on us!" Up on deck in our pajamas we saw that the sudden west wind was swinging us down on the rafted boats of the Mackinac fleet. I was horrified at the thought of colliding with those costly racing boats.

Half a dozen male voices shouted conflicting suggestions. Then we saw that *Gypsy*, a large power yacht, was drifting out of control over our anchor line. "Quick, cut your anchor line!" shouted a man who had leaped over onto our deck. I found a carving knife in the galley and sawed at the nylon rope. Then our anchor was gone— giving us a crazy, helpless feeling like a death in the family.

The rain seemed almost solid, ghost-lit by lightning. I closed all our hatches and ports as Carol and our neighbors secured us to the raft of boats. Changing out of our soaking pajamas, we tried to settle down for a few more hours of sleep, glad that we hadn't panicked in crisis.

By midmorning *Gypsy* motored back into harbor and handed us our anchor and line that they'd dragged out onto the lake, tangled in their own anchor. Carol rove it into our stub of anchor line and we felt relief! To be without an anchor is tricky, in sailing and in life.

Early in the trip, I lay awake at night in my narrow bunk listening to the wind in the stays and the squeak of rubber bumpers. Lying at or below water level, enclosed in liquid space, I felt as if I were in a womb. I lay with one leg poked out of my sleeping bag to keep in touch with the cool night air and deliberately handed over the crossing, and the future, to God. I can remember the actual moment. I was looking up at the small rectangular port, its glass faintly lit, and knew in my heart that though we needed to be alert and prudent, we didn't have to be in total control, that we could trust the Father to care for us and blaze a track against the wind, across those monster waves, all the way back to safe harbor at the end of the week. It was a moment of choice, and of growth because of choice.

The adventures continued with exhaustion, thunderstorms, winds, and the search for the line of land. And the relief of finally knowing our position, of having crossed, of prayers answered, settled on us like the calm of the water. By the final leg of our squared-off itinerary—from Egg Harbor back to home base at Sister Bay—we were up at six before any other boat in the harbor. We ghosted along without engine, in a gentle, one-knot air, floating like a tall insect over the silver surface.

The wind began to quicken as the sun got higher. Around Horseshoe Inlet it was fairly sizzling, and we were skimming along, heeling at seventeen degrees. This was our last ride, and it was thrilling to have this perfect sail.

We made a triumphant, letter-perfect entrance into the harbor —but no one was around to admire it. Except us. We stood inside ourselves and cheered, in awe at our dazzling performance!

For both of us, it was a time of risk in so many aspects of our lives: two women—single, though not by choice—facing lives that can be as clear or foggy, as sunny and calm, or as stormily fierce as Lake Michigan. We were learning to sail our life ships with charts, a compass, a depth sounder, and a wind that languishes and lifts by turns, unpredictable as the Spirit. But it is never a boring voyage.

Fullness of life in arenas of art and spirituality demands that we let go, that we relinquish control—something that goes against the human grain, particularly in a culture obsessed with empowerment. Here we are, trying to bring order and beauty out of chaos, gaining a kind of discipline and control, exercising the authority of experience and hard-won wisdom, and we have to *let it go?* How seemingly counterintuitive!

But it is in both the acceptance and use of the gift, and the giving it back that we find the rounding out of the process, the completion, the deepest fulfillment. We must give of ourselves to art, but we must accept that what we have to give is never enough, that for eternal significance any art, literature, music, drama must be Spirit-driven, Spirit-imprinted.

In his book *Finally Comes the Poet*, Walter Brueggemann writes that poetry is necessary to "disclose" truths that are "closed" by prose:

> Our technical way of thinking [which Brueggemann identifies with prose writing or preaching] reduces mystery to problem, transforms assurance to rigid certitude, revises quality into quantity, and so takes the categories of biblical faith and represents them in manageable shapes. . . . There is then no danger, no energy, no possibility, no opening for newness. . . . truth is greatly reduced. To address the issue of a truth greatly reduced requires us to be poets who speak against a prose world.[1]

So, for Brueggemann, art allows us to oppose the false clarity of oversimplification and disclose the truth in its diverse richness and complexity, its subtle nuance, which makes it less manageable but no less true.

In the context of control and manageability, the word *surrender* comes to mind—a word with somewhat negative connotations for me. It speaks too loudly of the sawdust trail, the guilt-charged evangelistic meetings of my youth. My word of choice is *abandon* —a wild and crazy word whose noun form is as powerful to me as its verb form.

In *Walking on Water*, Madeleine L'Engle writes that "to be an artist means to approach the light, and that means to let go our control, to allow our whole selves to be placed with absolute faith in that which is greater than we are."[2] And when God created us with free wills, *he* moved toward risk, letting go his control. When he became incarnate he relinquished the glory of heaven, giving his power away. But you know that story . . .

Growth. Creativity. By definition they are never static. All growth implies and requires change. And change suggests risk, a move into unknown territory, a step into the dark. This sounds dangerous, and it may certainly bring its perils with it, but it is also inevitable. Even those contented souls who find themselves at home with themselves in midlife—happy with their spouses, their circumstances, and their accomplishments, must face, along with the maturing of wisdom, the slow aging of the body and the constraints that accompany that shift. I am very aware that though my energy level and my motivation remain high, I am becoming more limited in my physical activities.

I can't climb mountain peaks like my sons can. I need a nap in the afternoon. The names of familiar, well-loved people sometimes escape me. From time to time I find myself unintentionally double-booking appointments. And I often search for a word that floats just above my rim of recollection.

But I don't ever want to stop growing, being creative. Even death, inevitable as it is, will be just one more creative spurt into the future, one more growing edge, one more leap into the light. Remember, we don't die into death. We die into life! As Floyd

Lotito said, "Death is not extinguishing the light; it is putting out the lamp, because the dawn has come."

Implicit within poetry (and any art that demands discipline) is also movement, vitality, freedom, and a certain unpredictability, an element of surprise. It is the startling, unexpected juxtapositions of words and ideas that are the most indelible. Poetry that is too rational, too controlled, too systematic, or too clear is as dull as water flowing through a pipe. What we want in writing is like the musical voice of river water encountering an obstacle—the angle of an upthrusting rock, the downward interference of a branch that results in a turbulence, a liquid clamor that calls the ear, a foam, a glittering ripple that snags the eye. All those watered wrinkles become prisms refracting the light. Such a dynamic art is unrepeatable and mysteriously satisfying.

James Gleick's fascinating book *Chaos* implies that as we penetrate the mysteries of matter, and some of the seemingly random activity of subatomic particles, another kind of microcosmic order and pattern becomes apparent. It seems a reaffirmation that it is the Word who holds all things together, whether or not we can discern the means or mechanisms of that order.

Think of the poetry of Dylan Thomas or Gerard Manley Hopkins. Much of their irresistible appeal lies in the force and wildness of their words and in their wantonness, their buoyancy, their refusal to be bound by convention. The poignant, raging despair of Thomas

and the ardent celebrations and desolations of Hopkins fuse earth
and heaven with an intensity as passionate as sex. They seem, often,
to mirror the fire and frenzy of creation itself, yet never randomly;
in their verses, form and chaos marry. But if (perish the thought!) it
were possible for us to smooth out their poems, civilize them,
make them genteel, clinical, and rational, hedge them around with
systems and safeguards and predictable rhythms, their feral vitality
would be snuffed out; rather than the savage grace of cougars, they
would display a safe, pussycat-like domesticity. William Blake
summed it up by saying that true "beauty is exuberance."

Ironically, the restrictions I have mentioned are those urged
upon the artist by the Christian community at large. For so long
as the risky and innovative aspects of art are retained, so long as
art mirrors the fervent creativity of a Creator who saw diverse
and beautiful creatures in his mind and then spoke them into
being, so long as art is what Eugene Peterson describes, in wholly
positive terms, as "subversive," the guardians of faith may refuse
it entrance to the holy precincts. Tame it, make it predictable and
palatable, overlay it with a veneer of orthodox respectability, erad-
icate its irony and wit, control its passion and force, and maybe,
maybe, it will be allowed to slip inside the sanctuary and be shown
to a back pew. The sterility of such a domesticated art shows us
the dire results of ultimate control.

Because the church has tended to fence off those parts of our lives
in which we feel danger, we are left with an attenuated view of life,
far from what God seems to have had in mind when he created us,
and far from a reflection of his own nature. By being indifferent to,

wary of, or even hostile to beauty, we've done a huge disservice to thoughtful people, and we've misrepresented our Creator.

We may despise beauty because we fear it. Perhaps we are afraid of a kind of idolatry, afraid that we may end up worshipping the created object rather than the Creator, afraid of losing control because we know that creativity doesn't always follow the rules.

The creative impulse is essentially innovative. It's always discovering new areas to explore. It experiments. It breaks down old barriers and ventures into unknown territory. That implies a kind of risk, and risk is something that many Christians are afraid of. "Coloring within the lines" requires a black-and-white system of belief and behavior, but I believe that when we control and hedge in certain parts of human experience, we end up being less than truly human. And truly human is the way God created us to be.

To see the kind of life God has in mind for us, we only have to look at Jesus and how he lived, constantly shocking the law-keepers and those around him, constantly coloring outside their lines. Scripture tells us "whatsoever things are of good report . . . think on these things"(Philippians 4:8 KJV), and we've assumed that that refers only to great moral truths. Somehow the church—in an effort toward control—has excluded beauty, when beauty is one of the greatest of moral essentials. Perhaps the role of those involved in the arts, then, is to awaken ourselves and others to beauty—in all its risk and in all its richness.

Chapter Nine

Paying Attention

I admire the way my thrifty New England mother-in-law used to bake. With a large family of children and grandchildren, she made bread several times a week using, along with her flour and yeast, whatever leftovers caught her fancy in the icebox that day: cold oatmeal, mashed potatoes, scrambled eggs, cottage cheese, or the baby's applesauce. Each time the bread emerged from the oven uniquely delicious, fragrant, and wholesome.

I want my writing to be like that. I want to start where I am and use what I have, and in the writing the mundane and trivial may show themselves to be of greater significance. All of the ordinary givens are fodder for my faith. I can grow and learn and worship within a humdrum context after a chance encounter.

God speaks from the loaves of bread, my granddaughter's watercolor of a rainbow, the buzz of a housefly, the smell of leaf smoke, a shell the shape of a baby's ear, the field flowers that border the highways. Each of them is a gift of grace.

These graces often begin with moments of attention and surprise. I was transfixed during a dinner party I was hosting for friends by the sudden sight in my dining room of a green vine spiraling up artistically out of the spout of a blue-and-white teapot as it sat on a shelf next to the wall. It had a surprised look, as if to inquire, "What am I doing here?"

Closer investigation (after the guests had departed) revealed its source as a dried pea hidden inside the teapot. My conjecture was that some time in the dim past, one of my young sons had been prodigal with his peashooter in the dining room, and the vagrant pea, nurtured at last by moisture of unknown origin, had been encouraged enough to sprout and wind its way in the dark toward the tiny star of light that shone through the teapot spout.

And the young plant shrouded in the soil "knows," senses, that its task is to reach the light. That it is destined for resurrection after its long burial—that to arrive in the light will mean life and health and fruitfulness.

Light is there for our seeing. Eyes and light working together result in sight.

One gospel reading in the Anglican lectionary that I recall from church months ago speaks to this. The reading came from Mark's gospel, chapter 10. It tells the story of blind Bartimaeus, who had the encounter of his life on the road out of Jericho. Hearing it read in church, sitting there in a pew, I was taken aback by the simplicity and urgency of the blind man's entreaty to Jesus—"I want to see" (v. 51 MSG), a request that I have been making on and off for most of my life.

All of us—artists, Christians—with a mission of living the truth that compels, of focusing the light and dispelling the darkness, acknowledge the need to *see*. And in order to see truly and deeply, we need to learn how to *pay attention* to both seen and unseen worlds.

The Sighting
John 9

Out of the shame of spittle,
the scratch of dirt,
he made an anointing.

Oh, it was an agony—the gravel
in the eye, the rude slime, the brittle
clay caked on the soft eyelid.

But with the hurt
light came leaping; in the shock & shine
abstracts took flesh & flew;

winged words like view & space,
shape & shade & green & sky,
bird & horizon & sun

turned real in a man's eye.
Thus was truth given a face
& dark dispelled, & healing done.[1]

Luci Shaw, *Polishing the Petoskey Stone*

How do we *see*? How can we condense into vivid words what we see? How, in the artist's life, can words and language be redeemed and abstracts "turned real"? How is "truth given a face"? How is the physiological faculty of *seeing* connected with the more profound insight—*in-sight*—of spiritual and intellectual perception? And what part has the human imagination in this play of glimpse and gleam, of hide and seek, of light and shadow? These are all questions in my mind.

Despite our present failure to know as we are known, to see with the clarity and breadth we long for, we need to remind ourselves of what Jesus told us: "If your eye is single, your whole body will be full of light" (Matthew 6:22, author's rendering). This implies a clear, sharp focus, without the blurring of myopia or double vision. Such seeing requires our deliberate, intentional joining-in-one of the separate images of our two eyes—a convergence. It calls us to be in a state of *attentiveness*.

For us to participate in the drama of creation presupposes our need to pay attention. (The word *pay* is significant—time and awareness, love, concentration and penetration are the price of seeing.) The details of God's creative activity are ubiquitous and all too often unnoticed. In Thomas Merton's words: "When the sun is always shining you forget that it is God's gift, and you don't pay attention anymore." But to ignore these evidences of God's magnanimity or view them as insignificant is to deny or demean the creative energy of God.

The word *attention* is derived from the Latin *ad-tendere*—"to stretch toward." Attending implies *inhabiting*. This is not a spectator sport. Paying attention cannot be done in passivity. It demands intentionality, choice, and awareness. And that, too, is costly. Especially in the gospel of John, the command, "Look!" draws our attention to significance. *Behold! Wow!* Christian spirituality demands that we stop in our tracks to see what's happening and to attend to it.

C. S. Lewis said, "Most of us miss our cues repeatedly." Or, as Sherlock Holmes commented to Watson: "You *see*, but you do not *observe*."[2] Artist Thomas La Duke noted: "Some things are so common that they disappear. They're all around us, but they vanish." Missing our cues, we fail to notice the fingerprints of the Creator in the ordinary textures and phenomena of living because we are distracted by daily urgencies, by things we consider more important, which in the end may prove to be both trivial and transient.

Mary Oliver wrote:

> *If you notice anything*
> *it leads you to notice*
> *more*
> *and more.*[3]

And here the incarnational approach to faith kicks in for me. As a poet and a sacramentalist, I am learning to recognize pointers to transcendent realities in almost anything I see. Thomas Aquinas put it like this: "We arrive at the knowledge of God from other things." It's not that we are inventing our own ideas about the Almighty but that we are exploring and examining the body of evidence already made available to us.

St. Paul recognized it in Romans 1:18. In Eugene Peterson's paraphrase *The Message*, it reads: "The basic reality of God is plain enough. Open your eyes and there it is! By taking a long and thoughtful look at what God has created, people have always been able to see what their eyes as such can't see: eternal power, for instance, and the mystery of his divine being" (vv. 19–20).

An impatient, often restless person, I've had to learn a great deal about slowing down, opening my eyes, paying attention, and waiting—often frustrating processes that seem like a waste of time. Yet as I read the Psalms, they are full of waiting: "Our soul waits for the Lord; He is our help and our shield"(33:20 NKJV). "I shall always wait in patience and shall praise you more and more." "Be strong and take heart and wait for the LORD"(27:14 NIV). "I lay my requests before you and wait in expectation"(5:3 NIV). "My soul waits for the Lord more than watchmen wait for the morning, more than watchmen wait for the morning" (130:6 NIV). (In that repeated phrase we feel the watchers' eager anticipation for daybreak after what seems like an endless night.) Waiting seems to be an inevitable part of the human condition, an inevitable part of the creative life.

Again, in the eighth chapter of the letter to the Romans, listen to Peterson's rendering of the apostle Paul's words about waiting:

> [Along with the creation in its birth pangs, waiting for its deliverance] waiting does not diminish us, any more than waiting diminishes a pregnant mother. We are enlarged in the waiting. We, of course, don't see what is enlarging us. But the longer we wait, the larger we become, and the more joyful our expectancy. (Romans 8:24–25 MSG)

If we have believed God's promise, if we have said yes to him as Mary did at the Annunciation, we are pregnant with God.

The promise of "Christ in you, the hope of glory" (Colossians 1:27 NKJV), though not physically visible, is truly being fulfilled in us.

During the waiting times God is vibrantly at work within us. And if through the Spirit of God we have been united with the Father in dynamic relationship, if God has sown his gospel seed in us, *then Jesus is being formed within us,* little by little, day by day. But we have to wait if the Word is to become flesh in us. And that kind of waiting feels like work.

"Don't you get tired of *noticing* things?"

A student leveled this question at me. Maybe some line of poetry had made her aware of something, disturbed her by something she'd never noticed before.

By way of answering her, I quoted one of my favorite sayings from Annie Dillard, embodied in a brief essay she wrote for *Life* magazine on, of all things, "The Meaning of Life": "We are here to abet Creation and to witness it, to notice each thing, so each thing gets noticed . . . so that Creation need not play to an empty house."[4] Dillard also said in *Pilgrim at Tinker Creek*, "Beauty and Grace are performed whether or not we sense them. The least we can do is try to be there."[5]

We cannot consume a six-course dinner in one gulp; to enjoy a meal to its fullest, we must savor every bite one savory morsel at a time. We cannot take in the whole universe at once. Every day gives us new chances for small discoveries, ways to view some commonplace object from a fresh angle, to acknowledge what Duns Scotus called *haeccitas*, the "this-ness," the "is-ness" of things;

to recognize what we already know but still need to learn, to detect the extraordinary in the ordinary. A move in the direction of this kind of awareness is a move toward a fresh appreciation of our richly detailed universe—the Creator's handiwork. The prime motivation for this exercise is curiosity; the prime requisites are time and focused attentiveness.

On my return from a two-and-a-half-week trip to the South Island of New Zealand, a land almost as unspoiled and uncongested as Eden, I reread a journal entry written during some memorable days I spent in the subtropical rain forest of the west coast. Most of the time I was alone, with camera and journal, intentionally opening my mental pores, as it were, to sensations and impressions. I wrote the following:

Journal Entry

True gratitude requires a concentrated awareness, a single eye, which is linked to recognition. Awareness, attentiveness, is something we all need to learn or relearn and to practice. Both these *A* words are linked with our ability to see. When we take the time, we find a kind of exhilaration in small things. My camera lens, with its zoom magnification, helps me to scrutinize what I might otherwise merely glance at and pass by. It becomes my other eye. When I frame and focus, I am also focusing my brain.

Here in the lushness of the rain forest I notice the microcosm of the moss gardens—minute, damp, velvet fronds like green sea anemones—small, low, unknown, unnamed greens. Green upon green upon green, lavish, even wanton in its rich diversity and texture. Diminutive starflowers scattered among the grasses. Tiny, uniformly polished and rounded stream pebbles, all the same shade of gray. The lacy, almost inky foliage of the New Zealand black birches.

My slowing down, stopping, being still, and listening allow me to hear the microcosm speak—the world of negligible, unnoticed things. We don't need to be world travelers or theologians or philosophers or environmentalists to see and hear the messages of heaven in the earthly creation. My magnifying lens is my tool for careful scrutiny.

Why the rich complexity and intricacy? Why pattern and the full spectrum of colors? The Creator is, like all artists, an experimenter, adding the grace of *beauty*, something nonessential in a pragmatic sense, but a clear reflection of what theologians call "grace." And each of us has a flash of that same aesthetic impulse, which needs only a modicum of human cultivation and expression to make us appreciative of the idiosyncrasies and surprises around us and send us off in our own creative directions.

We tend to think of the Creator in terms of the infinitely huge—mountains, continents, oceans, galaxies, universes, light-years. As the Almighty is beyond gender and time, so is he beyond size, glimpsed, if we open our eyes, in the helical unfolding of a shell, the lace of veins in a leaf with sunlight behind it, or as we penetrate deeper into physical realities, in the structures of sub-atomic particles, in the infinite unfolding of fractal patterns.

There's a surprising power in small things. Richard Wilbur, the great American poet, said it beautifully in his poem about a milkweed:

Anonymous as cherubs
Over the crib of God,
White seeds are floating
Out of my burst pod.
What power had I
Before I learned to yield?
Shatter me, great wind:
I shall possess the field.[6]

The milkweed pod or dandelion has immense power, enough to cover a whole hillside with new, young milkweeds, enough power to fill my lawn—and my neighbor's—with dandelions.

I'm reminded of the power of small things in Scripture, things that had large consequences: Individual lives or the fate of nations changing direction. The fruit eaten in the Garden of Eden. The olive leaf glimpsed in the beak of Noah's dove. The drops of lamb's blood painted over the doorways before the first Passover. The voice that the boy Samuel wakened to in the night. The "still, small voice" that arrested Elijah in his wilderness despair.

The bottomless vessel of oil that saved the widow and her family from starvation. For another widow, the handful of flour, which was all she had, but which she gave to the hungry prophet. The widow's farthing. The coin that Jesus found in the fish's mouth. A mustard seed, a single pearl, a sparrow, a hair on a human head.

Or of small events or incidents, which have altered the course of your own life. Never despise the power of small things, like seeds, to transform the landscape of the heart.

Throughout Scripture we continue to see the focus on the smallest details. In the Exodus story Yahweh's attention to detail is evident in the design and implementation of the Tabernacle. In

Exodus 28 we find an abundance of careful description and planning for the Tabernacle, and its furnishings and garments of the priests, that continues for pages.

God delights in the beauty of detail, in adornment. This is the very reason God wants his people to enjoy these details too. As Gene Edward Veith says in *The Gift of Art*:

> Beauty is an appropriate end in itself—the garments were to be made *for beauty*. The inventor of color, of form, of texture, the author of all natural beauties, values the aesthetic dimension for its own sake. According to the clear statements of Scripture, art has its place in the will of God.[7]

Francis Schaeffer has observed:

> The making of the Tabernacle involved almost every form of representational art known to humanity. But because God is also the God of creative imagination, of metaphor and symbol, of parable and analogy, the design of the Tabernacle, and later of the Temple, was packed with symbolism. The design and placement of furnishings and vessels, the use of different materials such as linen, goatskins, silver, brass, gold, acacia wood, and the ceremonies prescribed for the worship of God in these sacred precincts—the system of sacrifices and oblations—all had meaning *beyond themselves*.[8]

This is the essence of the sacramental: paying attention, noticing, discovering that material things remind us of—and point us to—the things we cannot see but that have ultimate and eternal reality and value.

God and his truth and beauty are like a sun that fills the sky. Huge verities flare off from its center like the flaming tongues of a corona, utterly overwhelming us in our insignificance. Yet, as with the inherent meaning of the materials of the Tabernacle, he may become visible to those who pay attention, whose eyes of belief and imagination are open, in a form as unthreatening and taken for granted as a baby or a dove or a lamb or a loaf of bread or a flick of prism color on a wall.

One day I stopped at the grocery store to get milk. When I came out, I realized I'd lost my new prescription sunglasses. I retraced my steps without result, talked to the store manager, left my phone number, and drove home with a heavy, frustrated feeling.

My one hope lay in knowing I had glued a sticker with my name and address on one arm of the glasses. It seemed a faint reason for optimism.

What made my loss doubly irritating was that these were the nicest bifocal, dark glasses I'd ever had: tortoiseshell, flattering (my mirror suggested), and a new prescription.

The next day I was watering the agapanthus in our front yard when I suddenly realized I had failed to ask the Lord's help in finding my glasses—I'd been unaware that they might represent something more significant.

"Lord, please restore my glasses," I prayed quickly. "And uncloud my inner lenses, my perception of you."

In the next moment, I heard a voice call to me from the driveway: "Is this 300 Menlo Oaks?"

"Sure is!" I called back as I walked toward an ancient Mexican man. He reached into his shirt pocket and pulled out my missing glasses. "I been looking for this street two hours." Broken English. Sweaty brow. No car parked nearby.

"Where do you live?" I asked.

"Gilroy" (a town nearly seventy miles south). "I come by bus."

"You came that far today?"

"Sí. I had to find you to give them back." He'd stood ahead of me at the checkout counter that day. Then he'd made a round trip of 140 miles to return a stranger's lost glasses!

I gave him a cool drink and cash for his bus fare, with some extra for his effort. I was indeed grateful for this act of kindness, this prayer answered.

I'm no apostle or prophet, but as a writer I take that command from Revelation 1 that the aging apostle John was told, "Don't be afraid. Write what you see" seriously. God has been telling me that all my life. In order to write truly, I need to see clearly; I need the right glasses.

A friend wrote to me, "Write what you can see and what you can't see." "What we can see" is what we can discern with our physical eyes. But God wants to fill our imaginations with realities for which we need inner, spiritual eyes, the kind of eyes that Jesus commended in some of his friends: "Blessed are your eyes because they see" (Matthew 13:16 NIV).

And the apostle Paul encouraged the Corinthians to look beyond the surface at "what is unseen. For what is seen is temporary, but what is unseen is eternal" (2 Corinthians 4:18 NIV). Divine lenses—God's vision given to us—make it possible for us to see both the visible and the invisible.

One spring in Illinois, my journal recorded a sudden weather change:

JOURNAL ENTRY

All the rain, sleet, melting ice, and warming southerly winds mean that there is too much water for the sodden ground to absorb—and there's no place for it to go. Every ditch and furrow and stream brims and glitters with water. As I travel the country roads, I see the sky reflected in places I've never seen it before.

Each night the temperature dips. Frost catches and controls the flooding until the next day. But during last night's darkness the level of the river dropped dramatically, leaving the saplings along its banks collared with lacy scallops of ice, with the black water churning away two feet below.

Contrasts—warm to cold, high to low, shadow to brightness, slick to rough—without each we lose the meaning of the other in this mortal life. Without struggle and storm, the smooth, sunlit days would dream along, serene and unremarkable, taken for granted. If on a scale of one to ten everything is a ten, then a ten has no meaning, except in heaven. It carries significance only if we contrast it with a one or a two. Without the dark, hopeless stretches in our emotional or spiritual seasons, we might get bored with blessing. Grace might seem stale.

Epiphany, the showing light, the revelation—perhaps its very transience is what lends it its appeal. If our days were routinely sun-filled, peaceful, tranquil, calm, predictable, and stress-free, their very serenity would soon seem flat, humdrum, monotonous, stale. God allows the darkness to be tempered by starlight, moonlight, a glow of approaching daylight. His summer warmth is such a relief from winter chill that we feel the difference with our skin and eyes and appreciate both light and warmth. There is purpose in the divine distinction between night and day, summer and winter, hot and cold.

William Stringfellow's perception that God makes himself known to us "here and there, now and then," strikes me forcibly as being exactly the way I experience God. It's not that he only comes to us "here and there, now and then," but that, distracted and preoccupied as we are—even with our *desire* to pay attention—we *perceive* him only sporadically, in bursts of intensity like an electrical power surge, rather than constantly—in a steady stream of light.

Have you ever bicycled along a country road overhung with foliage from thick woods on either side? As you rode, the sun pierced between the tree trunks, dappling you with sudden sunlight between stretches of deep shadow? You simply, at that moment, noticed a small thing: light on trees, on your skin. And yet there was more. Something deeper was startled.

God has a habit of surprising us with a vision of himself when we least expect it.

Chapter Ten

Cultivating Creativity

It has been raining hard for two days here in Sudden Valley. We've had at least four inches. The constant downpour has soaked the ground to a sog, and the ground, in turn, has drained like a full sponge into the creeks. My creek, Beaver Creek, has risen from its customary low summer profile of tea-dark water slow over pebbles (with the stream shallow enough so that the pebble tops poke, dry, above the surface) and has been supercharged with the overflow from the rain. All last night I heard it, my window open as usual to let in the wet sounds and fragrances. Often I could hardly tell in the dark if what I heard was heavy rain or rushing creek water or a liquid mix of both.

This morning the rain has stopped, but the stream is the color of caffe latte, twelve turbulent feet wide, and lapping at my house footings. The whole course of the creek bed, the gash along the bottom of this part of the valley, has changed. It is never static. Sometimes in August it almost stops, as if it is flowing cupful by cupful, carefully conserving itself during the dry months. But even that minimal movement is always fluid.

This creek is like my stream of consciousness. All day and all night it is in the background of my listening and thinking. It is there as I write or stoke the woodstove or sleep (dreaming) or make soup. Often I peer out at it through the window or step onto the deck to listen to it, as if I need to check it.

I think it is myself I am checking. Its flow is so like the flow of my own living or writing—slow and reflectively lazy sometimes or full and fierce in the rush of ideas and work. It is my metaphor—intensely personal. I am writing a stream. I am living a creek. I either feel the pebbles grazing my stomach as I swim or I half-drown in the torrent that follows the rain.

My other motif in this Sudden Valley life is the woodstove. Since I built this little house in the woods, I have had to learn about the care and feeding of stoves. With its chunky black iron body (attached to the ceiling and out to the sky by a sort of periscope, the chimney stack), the stove is like a small child. It requires constant attention and nourishment if it isn't to sulk and pant and go out on me, flames dying, embers cooling to a pile of nondescript ash and charcoal.

I attend to this phenomenon out of necessity rather than aesthetics but with the same kind of mythic consciousness as with the creek. Yes, I have electric baseboard heating, in obedience to the building code, but its outrageous expense drives me to the chopping of wood and the splitting of kindling—a messy, tedious, constant business, like writing. But like writing it is warming— once it is lit and going enthusiastically—to both body and soul.

Art, writing, takes time to get warm, to get going. Art takes concentration and sensitivity, too, which many are loath to give. Yet each of us possesses some kind of aesthetic response awaiting development—and development can be the tedious business. Like a sleeping child, it needs to be awakened, challenged, and exercised. Like a fire, attended to.

I envision a process something like this: Art is essentially inner, conceived in the artist's imaginative intelligence in response to the inspiration ("in-breathing") of a seed idea that, if it reflects truth, has ultimately been sown by God. Moving through a gestation period, this seed idea grows in the soil of the imagination, taking in nutrients from various sources, then flows from the mind to some arena outside the artist (the page, the word processor, the canvas, the stage, the musical instrument) where it is captured, crafted, and finally presented. At this point it assumes meaning for other creative intelligences who are nourished, delighted, and enlarged by the images. The creative idea has jumped the gap from mind to mind through art.

When the artist is a Christian, this seed idea will contain not only subjective meaning for its human creator but also objective truth related to its source—God himself. It will conform to what the artist knows of reality from the Christian perspective.

But true art neither moralizes nor preaches: its primary goal is not the spread of a doctrine or "message." No, art is in a different category. It is a qualitatively distinctive activity. Existing for the delight and illumination (through imagination as well as intelligence) of both artist and audience, it stands on its own—primary, independent, unique.

If art has a message, it is simply an acknowledgment that it reflects its source—the one who created and delights in all beauty and who transmits this imaginative impulse to his creatures. My responsibility as an artist is to stir up this gift, to exercise it, and to trust its direction and effectiveness to the one who gave it to me and into whose hand I have given my life.

For the Christian artist there will always be some attempt (also in nonverbal art forms such as sculpture, dance, mime, or instrumental music), to reduce anarchy to order; to reflect reality and moral/spiritual values, however indirectly; to contrast light with darkness, discord with harmony; to achieve a kind of balance; to give voice to an idea truthfully and with skill.

Today the terms *spiritual* and *spirituality* have a broad and hazy edge, implying a kind of sensitivity, an entry into a nonmaterial world of ideas and emotions. My masseuse describes herself as "spiritual." So does the young man who does my hair. I once had a Siamese cat whose mysterious comings and goings qualify him as a mystic. He even went *on retreat;* he spent his first days with me holed up behind the Bible commentaries in my bookcase— without doubt a *spiritual* feline. The French word *spirituelle* comes to mind. There is little intrinsically Christian implicit in the word.

On the other hand, my spiritual director, a fresh, earthy, intuitive, biblically literate woman, is one of the people with whom the traditional meaning of *spiritual* fits appropriately. Rooted as she is in Christ and impelled by Christ's Spirit, to be with her is to feel the divine presence.

This sounds comforting. Yet the reality is that Christian spirituality is much like the creative impulse of art—often fickle and unpredictable. We have an undomesticated God whom we cannot turn on and off like a water faucet.

This mystery, the spill of clues to an unseen reality, is very much a part of the artist's as well as the mystic's life. As a poet, as a thirsty Christian, I wait in silence by the sea or in the woods or more likely at my desk (with a deadline looming) for a poem to call me, claim me, write *me*, much as I wait in prayer for my God to speak his presence into me, to direct or correct me. I am not in control. I cannot turn on either poetry or the numinous like a light switch. My job, quite literally: to wait and see—to *wait*, and to *see*. And then if, or when, the epiphany is given, "to write what I see."

Neither art nor spirituality is a convenience, nor do they call to us at convenient times. If I am in conversation with a friend, a sudden insight or connection may turn me distracted. What is going on internally may have the intensity to switch my thoughts away from a casual greeting or discussion and make me wish my journal were handy so that I might catch this little jeweled insect before it flies away.

While creativity sometimes begins with seemingly random moments, it also sometimes begins with moments of epiphany.

For me, this has a lot to do with being in touch with the created world, where sometimes I am almost literally lifted out of myself. For example, it rained all day yesterday and then at sunset the sky cleared and everything was moist and glittering with wetness and smelled wonderful. I went out before supper and shot two rolls of film along the country roads around my home. It was so beautiful, I came home absolutely exhilarated. After the rain everything was incredibly glowing, yet earthy, as if heaven and earth were joined.

That type of experience gives me a tremendous boost in terms of art, because it's a sign that I am creatively responding to life.

The seed idea comes in a flash, and I try to record it, saving it to craft it later. I don't write every day, week, or month. I can't predict when that flash of insight will come. But it's important that I be listening and aware and receptive so that I can recognize the idea when it arrives and do something with it before it evaporates.

Unlike humanity at large, prophets and poets (and artists in general) seem to have been gifted in recognizing the idea and following it through, as the following confessions indicate.

Amy Lowell said:

There is a mystery here and no one is more conscious of it than the poet. Let us admit that a poet is something like a radio aerial—capable of receiving messages on waves of some sort and of transmitting them into those patterns of words we call poems. . . . A common phrase among poets is "it came to me." So hackneyed has this become that one learns to suppress the expression, but really it is the best description I know of the conscious arrival of a poem. . . . I do not hear a voice, but I do hear words pronounced, in my head, but with nobody speaking them. . . . Suddenly words are there, with an imperious insistence which brooks no delay. They must be written down immediately or an acute suffering comes on, a distress almost physical, which will not be relieved until the poem is given right of way. I never deny poems when they come; whatever I am doing or writing, I lay it aside and attend to the arriving poem.[1]

What an echo of Isaiah's "burden of the valley of vision" (22:1 KJV): the heavy message, the idea of urgent and primal significance that demands immediate communication.

Stephen Spender explained:

I have always felt that a poet's was a sacred vocation, like a saint's or a prophet's. . . . Everything in poetry is work except inspiration . . . inspiration is the beginning of a poem and its final goal. It is the first idea that drops into a poet's mind and the final idea which is at last achieved in words. . . . Writing poetry, when a poem appears to succeed, results in an intense physical excitement, a sense of release and ecstasy.[2]

Modest Mussorgsky, Russian composer of "Pictures at an Exhibition," wrote in his journal, "On a snowy day, seen through my window, suddenly appeared a colorful group of peasant women laughing and singing. The image this picture left on my mind became a musical form."

Igor Stravinsky described the process of creating his ballet *Petrouchka*: "In composing the music, I had in mind a distinct picture of a puppet, suddenly endowed with life, exasperating the patience of the orchestra with diabolical cascades of arpeggios!"[3]

Or look at Domenico Scarlatti's Fugue in G Minor, *The Cat's*

Fugue. The story is that Scarlatti's cat leaped up onto the piano keyboard in his studio and in walking along the keys struck a random and unlikely series of notes, out of which the composer fashioned his fugue. By a creative act Scarlatti brought order, beauty, grace, and meaning out of accident. And that is an act of redemption. Bringing order and beauty out of disorder or chaos, and meaning out of the meanest of circumstances, is God-work, in which we are called to be cocreators.

Or for another example closer to home, take a jumble of words to start with. On my refrigerator I have the collection of words on magnetic strips known as "Magnetic Poetry." From the hundreds of randomly scattered available words, several interesting ones seem to jump out at me from the metal surface, calling to be singled out: *sausage*, say, or *manipulate* or *repulsive*. Or *incubate*.

Icebox Poem

> *Dreaming,*
> *I shake the enormous moment,*
> *whisper static language into life,*
> *manipulate blue shadows in the sun,*
> *crush peaches for juice warm as blood,*
> *swim essential jungles,*
> *always incubate the image.*[4]

And here's a poetic rendering from my stepson, whose raging hormones infect the words that interest him!

> *The thousand goddesses—their*
> *delicate gowns ache after you*

> *like running light. Are they blowing*
> *roses, or kisses of death?*

You line them up. Strange juxtapositions and phrases that attract other words or prefixes or suffixes into their magnetic field. These surprising combinations of nouns and verbs with a few articles and conjunctions and a couple of adjectives paint a new picture or suggest some unplanned relationship that shifts or gels as other words are added or subtracted. *Order is overcoming randomness*, much as when Scarlatti's cat's strange, staggered, haphazard theme melted in the composer's mind and fingers and developed into a fugue with order, beauty, and meaning. As he felt a pattern emerging and followed its flow, out of randomness an order suggested itself.

For me as a poet, art is the impulse that gathers materials from almost anywhere in our rich, fragmented universe (even the fruit-and-vegetable section of my supermarket) and imposes a kind of lucidity, an order to the chaos, and finds significance everywhere. Art seems to be the product of our human impulse to find expression for that something within us that responds to our environment, which sees connections and cries out to be expressed, to reflect the meaning in beauty and vice versa.

Art is one of the lost healing things God has given us. There's this sense that *It's happened!* A magnificent sense of completion, of exhilaration, of lightness, which is wholly godly: God felt it when, after six days of creation, he shouted, "Good!" I feel that way when a poem is coming along and I know that it's right; when I'm read-

ing a line of it and have this certainty that it's really happening. It
may be a sort of affirmation after a period of drought, of not having it happen, so that when it does happen, it's profoundly satisfying and healing for the artist.

My hope is that here and there those who are ready can
reawaken that creative impulse, which I believe is universal.
Everybody is born with the ability to create in one form or the
other. If that can be restored or be reborn, it will heal and make
whole what may have been damaged or dulled. It does something
for the spirit—something we're not fully aware of. But when our
awareness wakens, we realize that in many ways art shares the
impulse of faith.

There is something radical about art and faith. Both are gifts.
Both are epiphanic—showings, manifestations. And both are
transformative—they change us. But it is in accepting the gift, stir-
ring it up, and then giving it back that we find the completion of the
creative process and a satisfaction akin to that felt by the Creator.

I've been working on a new poem. It started while I was driving
home from church one Sunday, thinking about making lunch, and
the asparagus that I'd bought the day before. I began wondering
about the word *asparagus*, speculating that it comes from the
Latin word *asperges*—"to sprinkle"—which is a term used in the
Episcopal or Catholic Church; there's actually a prayer, "Asperges
me, O God." Sprinkle me, God. So I start out: "O my asparagus
. . . O my avocado." And I'm talking to God. *Avocado* is the Spanish
word for "advocate." God's Spirit is our Advocate, the one who is
on my side to represent me to God. Then I got into spices and
flowers: "O my clove . . . O my carnation." Clove is from the

French word *clou,* a nail. I was thinking of the nails in Christ's flesh, and *carnation* speaks of flesh.

Incarnation is about being enfleshed. We're so familiar with red carnations, but we don't think of the *meaning* of the word. So I'm trying to get to the original intent of certain words and open them up. It never seems sacrilegious to be praying to God using these terms, because the original languages are so rich and full of meaning, which is why I'm grateful to have studied Latin, French, and Greek.

O *my asparagus,*
the cleansing sprinkle of your fern,
your stalked asperity under the melting butter; your gentle
      juices waken me to spring.

O *my avocado,*
your vegetable comfort calls my name,
teaching me the colors of green. And your purpled leather rind
      discloses a sumptuous spirit around your oily seed heart.

O *my small clove,*
your dark nail probes my hand studding my open palm like a
      pink Easter ham,
pinning me to Christ's last clench of pain.

O *my scarlet carnation,*
your iron-fresh scent, and the sharp, pinked edges of your dying
      outflesh for me the colors
of God's blood, God's body.

O *my pear . . .*

I never quite completed this outpouring, but I recognized it as a personal psalm, if you like, a contemporary psalm. I don't know if it'll ever become a finished poem, but it's a beginning, and it will build on itself.

Art begins here: with fragmentary thoughts that keep coming. Your mind functions as a percolator; art bubbles up in the back of your mind even when you're not conscious of it. It's an interesting process, cultivating an idea; I find if I have a problem or something that needs resolution, I can "feed" it into my mind at night and expect an answer in the morning. Very often by then something has become clear without my conscious cogitation. Artists know it to be a secret process. It's fascinating to me that the human mind has that capacity. And I believe that it's the work of the Spirit.

Though there are many gifts, showings, or a seemingly random grouping of words that come together, still, there are no shortcuts to becoming good at one's craft. Where to begin? First of all, with a sense that you have a gift, an understanding for words, a feeling for rhythm in language.

I think what helped me most was having a family that read aloud—books, lots of books. Biblical books, but also some of the great masterpieces of fiction. When we were children, we were used to reading aloud and hearing language in its most dynamic form, and that fed something in us that quickened the imagination. We learned firsthand how language works.

The other thing that helps the writing craft is to write, and write, and rewrite. You learn to write by writing. I don't know any tricks or special techniques—I suppose there are some basic rules to follow, but it's one of those gifts you can't develop without *doing* it.

Students often want to be "made" into poets, and they view it as a rather passive activity: "Well, I'll just take your course," they say, "do what you tell me. I'll follow the rules—learn to be a poet." But there has to be something that springs from within you that burns in you and wants to be alive, and expressed.

So how do we grow in our craft? One way is to read in our artistic fields. I read a great deal of contemporary poetry. I have shelves and shelves of poetry, and I read many literary magazines. I'm always watching for new trends, new techniques, different poetic styles, experimentation. Even though experimentation doesn't always "work," it's for my writing to keep those edges growing.

We grow, too, by affirming our loves through craft. Much of my work is centered in the natural creation, my love for the wilderness. It may have had something to do with my growing up; our summers were spent in the Muskoka Lakes in northern Ontario where I went to camp every summer. Just being able to be in the woods is very conducive to reflection, as is floating in my canoe just under the overhanging maples, with the water lapping at mossy boulders.

There's something about green and growing things that absolutely clutches at me; nature becomes like a second Bible. In fact, it's hard for me to read Scripture freshly. It is not that it has lost its value—and I'm so committed to it—but I've grown up with it in my ears; I'm so familiar with it that sometimes I get more of a fresh sense of God's presence and significance in the natural world. Theologically, nature is recognized as a secondary revelation of God—the Scriptures and Christ being the primary revelations.

From there we take our craft as response. For me, my writing is a connection with the world, my response to the world around me. As William Stafford said, "Love calls us to the things of this world." And I think most good art has to be conceived through personal experience. It has to be concrete and individual; if it's theoretical, it loses its punch.

Craft, for the writer, is always informed by reading—observing others in their craft, which in turn inspires our own. I've collected a substantial library of contemporary and traditional poetry and fiction. When I feel dry as an artist, the best way for me to prime the pump is to read the work of other poets. I'm not plagiarizing or parroting their ideas, but the flow of their words and images pulls me into my own fresh writing.

I'm an omnivorous reader, with an untidy pile of diverse books and journals on my night table—biography, travel, literary fiction, poetry, memoirs, devotional readings, essays, the Bible, the Book of Common Prayer.

Books are perhaps my most meaningful resource, this community of friends on my shelves, each volume bursting with the author's originality and penetration. These are ones to be read, reread, loaned to friends, treasured, and mourned over when lost. Books like Annie Dillard's *Holy the Firm*, Jane Kenyon's *Otherwise*, Seamus Heaney's *The Spirit Level*. Hopkins and Hudgens, Herbert and Rilke and Frost, Kinnell and Olds, Oliver and Levertov, Rumi and Schnackenberg and R. S. Thomas. In the arid spells that sometimes beset me, this is a community of refreshment and rekindling of some little internal flame. To change the metaphor, reading language that sings and resonates, I myself begin again to feel like a bell.

Among the things that good literature involves are elements of inevitability and surprise—essential to all arts. A well-wrought work gives the sense that this is the way it was inevitably *meant to be*, and part of that certainty comes from the surprises in it, words in unusual juxtaposition, fresh ideas that give us a little jolt of astonishment.

Yet there is another community that informs the creative life: friendship, which is formed with others who share a conviction of faith and a dedication to artistic process.

On the Meyers-Briggs personality scale, I always come out balanced on the cusp of E and I—extroverted and introverted. Being with engaging people is for me both energizing and exhausting. The conversations get intense, the relationships heat up, ideas pop like champagne. I end up exuberant but overstimulated and too wired to sleep. My emotions feel rubbed raw. At that point I tell my convivial husband, "I need time alone."

Uninterrupted solitude feels as good as a massage. In the woods in a tent, maybe, or walking a beach looking for some perfect stone. And a kind of restoration begins. At which point I can rejoin the human community with some degree of equilibrium.

With an impressive resume in busyness drawn from my zealous evangelical upbringing, the benefits of meditation, silence, and aloneness—of listening to the Spirit in these ways—are new discoveries for me. Yet without people in my life, I would be impoverished. Especially as a writer, needing long stretches of days without phone, e-mail, or other techno-conveniences, there is still a part of me that relishes human interaction. And this is another way that fresh ideas form, that creativity is challenged and renewed: through community.

This can happen in several contexts for me—a flourishing church community, my church choir, my children who live nearby, a weekly group of women who open up our lives for prayer with each other. These are mixes rich as fruitcake, where love and fellow feeling learn to overlook individual flaws and celebrate life successes and blessings of our friends, while standing with them in the kinds of crisis or failure to which we all fall victim.

About the community of faith, Annie Dillard writes: "There's order, and there's beauty, and you're taken away from yourself . . . You're taking a stand with these people. You're saying: 'Here I am. One of the people who love God.' . . . I don't see the church as a series of rules. I see it as a body of believers."

As an Episcopalian, I participate in my church's fairly structured liturgy, which is theologically very orthodox. It makes room for the beauty of architecture and music and the sacramental approach to life (in which everything temporal is a pointer to something eternal). But if I find kindred spirits in my church whose poetic or artistic life is not being fed, and who are really lonely and hungry for creative companionship, I might stand up during church announcements and invite such people to a potluck at my house where we can talk about creative ways to express our love for God and each other.

I am surprised at how an artistic community begins to form.

This community, then, may break up into smaller groups that reflect its diversity. Painters in one group, writers in another, actors or musicians in another. In one church we started a yearly arts festival where a play was performed, a concert given, or an exhibition of photography and painting staged. The consciousness of the church as a whole was raised to recognize the importance and significance of art as a way to worship and serve God.

In church and outside of it, Communion and community bond. Each small slice of life becomes sacramental as we acknowledge our humanity and pray together for God to be made flesh in us. At the altar for Eucharist, no matter our political leanings or past history, we meet in the presence of the one who draws us together as parts of one body—those who have died, those with whom we live and work, and those yet to be born—we're all part of the family—the communion of saints. Christ's body and blood become the food and drink of life and growth. And in turn we become his fingers and his feet.

My husband, John, and I are committed to that sense of encouragement and family. We have a monthly discussion group in our home that approaches many different topics: science, faith, the arts, politics, ethics, adventure, film, and so on. We'll bring in a speaker or an artist or a writer to talk about his or her area of experience and then invite questions and discussion. By being exposed to this rich mix of ideas, most people find an area of interest into which they can grow.

Every human being is gifted with some kind of creativity, but all too often it has had no opportunity to develop. I think this is where creative leadership on the part of pastors and church staff can begin to foster and encourage artistic gifts and growth.

In my writing life, it used to be that I resisted the idea of showing early work to anyone, as if that might squander something concentrated and precious, like Onan spilling his seed in the Old Testament story. Or like spreading a resource too thin—a stream meant to be directed into one forceful channel diverted into a shallow, meandering oxbow of a river.

But being part of a community of like-minded writers—readers with perceptive eyes and ears—has become vital for me as a poet. Because each of us writes alone, and in the writing gets far too close to our own poems and essays to be objective about their flaws or possibilities, and because we sometimes get stuck, we need the community of other poets we know and trust, whose eyes and finely tuned sensibilities can detect a gap in logic, an awkward line, a failure in consistency, a false tone. Such colleagues might say, "This poem begins strongly but peters out. Why don't you end it after the third stanza?" Or "Remarkable image, that." Or "I like where this is going" (a kind way of indicating that it hasn't quite arrived there yet).

Many artists feel very isolated, very alone. They feel as Elijah felt: "I alone am left" (1 Kings 19:14 NASB). I'm all alone, no one else feels what I'm feeling or understands what I'm doing. But I have been fortunate; I belong to a group of writers called the Chrysostom Society. There are twenty of us (and our spouses), and we get together once a year. We've been doing this now for many years. It's a great support system, where we work through very practical problems of writing issues, among other things. Our group meets many needs each of us has felt. We have developed deep friendships, intentional friendships, through this group, relationships that continue between our formal gatherings.

We all share a fairly similar worldview. The goal of the group is to encourage each other's writing so that each of us is doing better work. We feel that many Christians have the reputation of doing mediocre work compared to some of the giants in the secular world. Our hope is that we can do work that compares favorably with any writer, Christian or not, so that Christians can become acknowledged in this wider arena. And we have that as a goal. Fifty years ago, the goal of writers who were Christians was to write *good theology*. Now that's being joined and partnered with the idea of *good writing*. The two need to work together.

I'm also part of a writers group that meets every other week. We slash and bash each other's work and bow to the blows when they come our way, which can be salutary, if painful. There is occasional applause. This is one tough bunch; we all acknowledge the power of regular work shopping to raise the level of competency and lyricism. It also heightens our awareness, keeps us answerable to our peers, and renders us more prolific than if we never had the courage to bare our souls, and our writing, to other poets.

I also send out early drafts of poems by e-mail to a friend on another coast and to one in another country. And they send their new work to me for comment and critique.

Following the advice of Donald Hall, a fine American poet, we are ambitious, not so much for ourselves, but for our work—that it will end up being what it was meant to be; that it will teach us what we hadn't figured out on our own; that it will say something fresh and vivid and surprising to our readers; that it will contribute some vital component to a culture too often stultified and barren.

Chapter Eleven

Understanding the Shadow Side of Creativity

$\mathcal{S}$ometimes it almost seems as if God is capricious, showing himself openly from time to time. This is most purposefully and powerfully seen in the Incarnation. And then at other times, God seems to hide himself, "dwelling in darkness," in what seems to our human perception an arbitrary way.

I wrote the following poem in Christ Church Cathedral in Oxford, in the small, decrepit chapel of an eighth-century saint who was the patron saint of Oxford. Every other part of the cathedral had been beautifully restored, but the poem tells the story of this chapel's age and neglect and of my own longing to make sense of the fragmentary ceiling fresco:

St. Frideswide's Chapel

In this ancient place
one section of the fresco
ceiling has been left
to peel, a puzzle, half
the pieces lost. As from
the bottom of a well I stare
up, waiting for revelation.
A raw plaster frowns
from the past, a closed sky, murky
as thunder, traced with

gold shreds—a snatch
of hair, a broken chin line,
wing fragments in red, in blue.
My eyes are busy—deepening
pigment, filling in the detail
of hands, feathers, touching up
the face of an angel. But nothing
changes. The terrible inscrutability
endures, deeper than
groined arches. Tattered

seraphim flash their diminishing
edges, like the chiaroscuro God who,
if we believe Michelangelo, touched
Adam into being with one finger,
whose footprints crease the blackness
of Gennesaret, whose wing feathers

brush our vaulted heaven, purple
with storm, whose moon
is smudged—a round, glass window,
an eye moving between clouds.

The God who is not there. Or, the God who is *there* but not *here,* except for occasional momentary visitations. I have often felt, in reflective moments as well as at the raw edge of experience, that I have a now-you-see-him, now-you-don't God, a chiaroscuro God, some of whose features are highlighted in the manner of the Italian Renaissance painters who employed that technique but whose being exhibits such mystery, such inscrutability, such otherness that it can only be represented by deep shadow, which might as well signal absence as obscurity, it is so unknowable.

The word *chiaroscuro* is itself an oxymoron—*chiaro* (clear, or light) combined with *oscuro* (dark), suggesting ambiguity and paradox, a fitting term for a deity who has revealed himself in the flesh yet walks in mystery, who scatters clues and hints to his being throughout creation, Holy Scripture, and the human mind, leaving his burning footprints on the lake, but then withdrawing.

And we are supposed to *trust our lives* to this enigma? All very well for the author of *The Cloud of Unknowing,* but what of those of us who are pragmatic realists rather than mystics? And am I the only one who feels puzzled and in jeopardy because of this conundrum?

We yearn for union with God, for the sense of safety and belonging. What we often experience instead is frustration and aloneness. Psychologist and theologian Gerald May spoke to this tension:

We have this idea that everyone should be totally independent, totally whole, totally together spiritually, and totally fulfilled. That is a myth. In reality, our lack of fulfillment is the most precious gift we have. It is the source of our passion, our creativity, our search for God. All the best of life comes out of *our human yearning —our not being satisfied.* Certainly Scripture and religious tradition point out that we are not to be satisfied. We are meant to go on looking and seeking.[1]

Oh, yes! I find myself thinking. *That's it exactly. It's the* longing *to know who God is that draws us like a magnet.*

If all I know is sunlight without shadow, will I fail to appreciate it? Might I even feel bored with the monotony of continuous light? It's the darkness that causes me to question and to search.

Gerald May's ideas bring me some comfort. But I would go even further. In studying the Beatitude that describes the blessing of being hungry and thirsty for righteousness, I have wondered if that hunger and thirst had something to do with the longing C. S. Lewis talked about—*sehnsucht,* the desire to experience some poignant, holy, intangible beauty that is indescribable but for the conviction that when we find it the joy will make sense of all the heartache and darkness and emptiness of our present existence.

Sometimes, and again I speak from personal experience, the feeding of our hunger and the slaking of our thirst feels agonizingly slow. There are seasons when God seems to impart himself to me, as in the Eucharist—a crumb, a sip, allowing me just enough of himself, just enough nourishment to keep me alive.

Ron Hansen, in *Mariette in Ecstasy,* suggests:

How important it is for God to be away from us and be the one we pine for but cannot have, for *desiring God invigorates,* desiring him but never fully having him we cannot grow tired or slack. We know the joy of "hereness" now and then, but were his distance and indifference all we had, it would still be sufficient if we sought and cherished it.[2]

Blaise Pascal told us that "a religion which does not affirm that God is hidden is not true." *Vere tu es Deus absconditus.* Even the Annunciation, that announcement of the arrival of Light into the world, had its shadow side. In Greek the language is plain. The angel spoke prophetically to Mary in the gospel of Luke, telling her, "The power of the Most High will *overshadow* you" (Luke 1:35 NIV).

Cleopas and his friend, on the way to Emmaus in the days following the Crucifixion, were perplexed about Jesus's fate and disappearance—Jesus, who had been their hope for Israel and its liberation, was no longer with them. The reason for hope had vanished. Then Jesus showed up *incognito* and walked with them, even breaking bread with them, but at the moment when "their eyes were opened and they recognized him" (Luke 24:31 RSV), he disappeared from their sight. As soon as they understood, he was gone!

God's greatest acts may leave us hanging. We, like those friends of Jesus, have glimpses of knowing, of seeing something transcendent that confirms our faith. But because it is *faith*—which has to do with things not yet seen—we also must live with the biblical experience of feeling left in the lurch.

Is this all by divine design? Can I affirm with C. S. Lewis that "my best havings are wantings"? In a letter, Lewis wrote: "All joy (as distinct from mere pleasure, still more amusement) emphasizes our pilgrim status; always reminds, beckons, awakens desire. Our best havings are wantings."[3]

The poignant desire for God is part of the awakening of the moral and the creative imagination. There is a thrill and an agony to it, a void created in us by the suction of vacuum—much like the gravitational pull of the sun upon our small planet.

In *The Problem of Pain*, Lewis (quoting him yet again—as he speaks so lucidly to these large questions) comes even closer to this feeling of being earthbound yet magnetized by heaven and its promises:

> There have been times when I think we do not desire heaven; but more often I find myself wondering whether, in our heart of hearts, we have ever desired anything else. . . . It is the secret signature of each soul, the incommunicable and unappeasable want, the thing we desired before we met our wives or made our friends or chose our work, and which we shall still desire on our deathbeds.[4]

So. We live, still amphibious, in a place of faith and prophetic hope. The darkness, the hunger, the thirst, and the desire all make a void, a vacuum by which our hearts are inevitably drawn toward the fulfillment of that want. We glimpse the transcendent momentarily. As artists, we explore it in the temporal hiatus between fierce desire and realization that we live in hope until we are sprung from the trap like birds released from a cage into the limitless sky; until the end of the matter, whose eternal timing only God knows.

Art, with all its desire and amphibious nature, can never reflect simply sweet reasonableness. In the hands of a Christian artist, it may be consciously outrageous, a creative statement as deliberately hyperbolic as Jesus's statement in the gospel of Matthew: "If

your right hand causes you to sin, cut it off and throw it away"
(Matthew 5:30 NIV). Such art is meant to jolt, to shock, to sting, to
press truth into our awareness in unforgettable ways.

Often, however, art is veiled—couched in clues and symbols, a
shadow that touches reality, that gives us a glimpse of the indescribable, that invites us farther up and farther in. It will not always
show all of itself or the whole truth at one viewing, nor will it
preach a four-point sermon. But if we are willing to give it our
attention, art will begin to open our inner eyes.

By breaking the rules, crossing the preordained boundary, attempting to seize control in the divine-human relationship, our first parents bequeathed to us the legacy of chaos. We find it within
ourselves, to our dismay, that spirit battles with flesh; our two
natures are at war.

Yet along with our internal conflict, we are conscious of what
Lewis called "the longing for a form"—that pattern created in us,
the Spirit dwelling within us as in a holy place, to give meaning
and purpose to life and art, to provide the essential and internal
discipline that makes beauty and enthusiasm ("in-goddedness")
possible. The danger is that we will be satisfied instead with the
external control of artificial restriction, the human legalisms that
make it seem safe to play the game of life.

But for those who take faith and art seriously, consider the strat-
egy of not playing it safe. Artists particularly know that the bright-
est gleam of human, natural, or spiritual beauty of ecstasy is shot
through with shadow; it is temporal, fleeting. For all her lucid per-
ceptions, Emily Dickinson felt a lifelong, unfulfilled ache for faith.

Art often speaks to us *subliminally,* sub-liminally, "below the threshold" of our conscious awareness. *Limen* is Latin for *threshold* and is often applied in connection with the kind of knowledge that comes to us in ways that bypass our cognitive reasoning and our senses. In that regard, art—poetry, music, painting, dance, drama—helps us to see the unseeable and know the unknowable, ushering us into the realm of the transcendent.

For example, on a stormy night the power goes out all across town. Your own house is without light, and you are left stumbling around in the pitch dark, trying to remember where you left the flashlight, or at least some matches and a candle. The lack of light makes you most powerfully aware of its necessity for your life and well-being. The missing element is the one of whose reality you are most aware. Absent though it is, the reality of light attracts you like a moth to a candle.

It was out of a time of absence, an intense but unfulfilled desire to know God in the continuing present, that I wrote the book *God in the Dark,* filled with the questions that came with the crucible experiences of my husband's terminal illness and my bereavement. Forgive me for quoting out of my own book.

> I've been thinking of the cloud which covered Jesus and the disciples during the Transfiguration—that "cloud of unknowing" which blocked our Lord from their sight. It seems that if we are disciples who want to be close to Jesus, we must go through that

cloud, or wait for it to lift and the Father to show us the Son. Meanwhile, we live blinded by the dense fog on the way up the mountain.

Further on:

How the world seems to be divided into a dualism of light and darkness! We usually associate God with the light, especially in Jesus, "the light that shines in the darkness and is not overcome by it," "the light that lights everyone who comes into the world." But when the Father turned the light of his face away, Jesus was left hanging in the deep shadow, crying over the agony of his abandonment.

And Jehovah himself, in his mystery, his terrible otherness, has often seemed to be dark. Solomon voiced his realization that "the Lord has said that he would dwell in thick darkness" (2 Chronicles 6:1). But out of that enigmatic cloud there flashes from time to time "the downward dart of lightning."[5]

Blaise Pascal, in *Pensées* 446, said:

If there were no obscurity, man would not feel his corruption; if there were no light, man could not hope for a cure. Thus it is not only right but useful for us that God should partly be concealed and partly revealed, since it is equally dangerous for man to know God without knowing his own wretchedness as to know his wretchedness without knowing God.

And of course there are encouragements toward perseverance, such as the words of this hymn:

Hope on then, broken spirit,
Hope on, be not afraid.
Fear not the griefs that plague thee
And keep thy heart dismayed.
Thy God in his great mercy
Will save thee, hold thee fast,
And in his own time grant thee
The sun of joy at last.

And this verse from the epistle to the Romans: "If we hope for what we do not yet have, we wait for it patiently" (Romans 8:25 NIV).

Sometimes, and I speak once again from personal experience, the waiting, the feeding of our hunger, feels agonizingly slow. Sometimes I have wondered if I will die of heart-hunger. Sometimes I am Hansel or Gretel following the sparse trail of crumbs to find home.

What We Say We Want

What do we say when
that hunger harrows our bodies?

I desire you. But it's not
that, or not only that.

Desire is the word we use as an excuse
for all the pain, a white flag
dropped into the battle that rages
between urgency and fulfillment.

A time of exhaustion comes
when nothing is left to want;

or when what we still want
is too large to name.

Even physical, sexual desire is only an echo of the huge wanting that consumes us, which is never satisfied this side of heaven—the desire to know someone to the fullest, a clenching of two bodies, two souls, the need for a supreme and burning intimacy.

The Psalms and Prophets are full of expressions of longing, of looking and seeking. "I long for you, in an arid, exhausting land where there is no water" (Psalm 63:1, author's rendering). This kind of hunger and thirst has a kind of gravitational pull, an energy field that excites and draws us like a magnet toward that final translation of body and soul into the realm where, as Lewis compellingly described it in *The Great Divorce,* ultimate reality dwells.

The author of *The Cloud of Unknowing* voiced the intensity felt by unfulfilled seekers after God: "Smite upon the thick cloud of unknowing with the sharp dart of longing love; come what may, do not give up."[6]

Dietrich Bonhoeffer in his *Testament to Freedom,* wrote in reference to Psalm 42:1:

"As a hart longs for flowing streams, so longs my soul for Thee, O God."

Have you ever, on a cold autumn night in the forest, heard the piercing cry of a deer? The whole forest shudders with the cry of longing. In the same way here, a human soul longs, not for some earthly good, but for God. Godly persons, whose God has removed himself from them, long for

the God of salvation and grace. They know the God they long for; here are
no seekers after an unknown God who will never find anything. At some
time they have experienced God's help and nearness.

Thus they do not cry into a void.

But even presence does not mean vision. In Exodus we read,
"Moses approached the *thick darkness where God was*" (Exodus 20:21
NIV, italics mine). Moses waited forty days and nights on the mountain before he was given a glimpse of Yahweh's "back parts"(Exodus
33:23 KJV).

Of course, the "absent" God may prove to be merely the hidden God. The writer of the Proverbs gave us this paradox: "It is
the glory of God to conceal a matter" (Proverbs 25:2 NIV).

Some believe that God is hidden only to hardened sinners. Yet
"the dark night of the soul," the absence or darkness of God experienced by myriad dedicated, tenacious Christians and holy saints,
such as St. Teresa of Avila and St. John of the Cross, is a common
enough experience to be recognizable to most of us. Another
related description of this isolation from God is "the winter of the
heart," in which the heart feels frozen but continues to wait for the
arrival of spring.

Belief somehow falls short of knowledge, of firsthand experiential certainty. When we say of someone, "I believe she'll be in
later this afternoon," we mean, "I'm not sure. It hasn't happened
yet. But I hope—" Belief is private, personal, hidden within the
small comet of the heart, as against the public universe of all that
which is known and knowable. Belief is like the excitement of fire-
works, the explosion of light and sound clearly visible and audible
against the silence of a night sky, which dies away and leaves us
once again in the quiet darkness. Knowledge is like the slow, steady

burn of sunlight through a window.

St. Anselm said, "I believe in order to understand," *Credo ut intelligam.*

Our Guide is the Holy Spirit—through whom we feel that a baptized, or redeemed, imagination is an imagination that is truly listening for God images. And for truth.

But truth isn't always pleasant. Christians who practice art must not always feel bound to produce sweetness and light. We have to recognize the darkness and shadow as well as the light, and realize that God allows shadows into our lives. God is not dark and evil, but he embodies mystery.

Sometimes God withdraws and leaves us in the dark—and we can learn to view it as an instructive and salutary phase of life. It's not pleasant, but we discover things in the dark that we wouldn't find in the light. The contrast between darkness and light is important: the light shows the darkness for what it is, and the dark shows the light for what it is. Contrast highlights, as it were; it allows meaning to be seen and experienced.

Often I have felt this strength of being "carried along," like a small boat in a flowing current, by the community of faith—even as I feel I am in darkness. Every week at the eucharistic feast, I participate in the old exchange: at Communion I bring to the altar all my flaws and failings, handing over to God my fears and skepticism and inadequacy, and Christ offers me himself instead, feeding me body and blood, his food for my soul, which strengthens me for the journey of the coming week as I "feed on him in my heart, by faith."

Kneeling at the Communion rail, I feel like a little bird being fed crumb by crumb from God's infinite loaf, to keep me going until the next sacramental meal.

John Stott, the venerable and deeply orthodox Anglican priest and writer, was quoted in *Christianity Today*: "The invisibility of God is a great problem."[7] Why is truth so often presented as mystery? Isaiah cried out, in seeming frustration, "Verily thou art a God that hidest thyself"(Isaiah 45:15 KJV).

Even in the New Testament, apart from the Revelation consisting mainly of historical narrative and hortatory teaching, mystery abounds. It is defined as something secret, hidden, not known to all—though gradually revealed. There is the "mystery of iniquity," the "mystery of godliness," the "mystery of the gospel," and the "mystery of the kingdom." There is the "mystery of marriage"— between man and woman, and between Christ and the Church— and the "mystery of Jew and Gentile united as one body in Christ." There are others. All mystery feels like fog. It presents hiddenness. It demands strong faith to walk into it believing that one day it will be demystified.

Still I return, mystery and all, like a bird to the eucharistic table, fed crumb by crumb, because even in mystery, revelation is enacted.

The news we feed on at the table of God is that God is known to us as the revealer of "hidden" things. We're familiar with the startling aria from Handel's *Messiah*, "Behold, I show you a mystery." Life after death in a transformed body. Or the mystery of "Christ in you, the hope of glory" (Colossians 1:27 KJV), truths not known before, planned by God but hidden until his chosen time of revelation (Daniel 2:22).

Despite what we know of darkness, God is still in the business of revealing hidden things. In the second chapter of the Acts of the Apostles, we read, "In the last days," God said, "I will pour out my Spirit upon all people. Your sons and daughters will prophesy, your young men will see visions, your old men will dream dreams. Even on my servants, both men and women, I will pour out my Spirit in those days and they will prophesy" (vv. 17–18 NIV).

Within the revelation of hidden things are visions, alternate views of supernatural reality. The writer of Proverbs put it this way: "Where there is no vision, the people perish"(Proverbs 29:18 KJV). Vision is as necessary to the human spirit as food is to the human body.

People who see symbolic visions from God, who hear his words and utter his oracles, are called prophets. Poets, creative writers, musicians, artists, all the creators are gifted with insight, imagination, and the ability to express themselves in symbols and figurative language—often appearing within their cultures and times as prophets, as voices calling in the wilderness. The revelation to John on Patmos is an example of this kind of symbolic vision. He wrote:

> I was in the spirit on the Lord's day, and I heard behind me a loud voice like a trumpet saying, *"Write* in a book *what you see* and send it to the seven churches. . . ." Then I turned to see whose voice it was that it spoke to me, and on turning I saw seven golden lampstands I saw and in the midst of the lampstands I saw one like the Son of Man, clothed with a long robe and with a golden sash

across his chest. His head and his hair were white as white wool, white as snow; his eyes were like a flame of fire, his feet were like burnished bronze, refined as in a furnace, and his voice was like the sound of many waters. In his right hand he held seven stars, and from his mouth came a sharp, two-edged sword, and his face was like the sun shining with full force. When I saw him, I fell at his feet as though dead. But he placed his right hand on me, saying, "Do not be afraid . . . write what you have seen" (Revelation 1:10–19 NRSV, italics mine).

The words *seer* and *prophet* describe the double identity of the biblical spokesperson who *sees,* looking toward heaven, receiving the vision, and who *prophesies* to earth, proclaiming the oracle. Christian poets stand with the seer and prophet, one foot in heaven, one on earth, perpetually torn by that duality of focus as the divine dream is channeled through their human voice or pen. The mandate to John on Patmos—"Write what you have seen"— is the root from which, consciously or unconsciously, all imaginative writing springs.

Flannery O'Connor described the function of the prophet in the church like this: "According to St. Thomas, prophetic vision is not only a matter of seeing clearly, but of seeing what is distant, hidden. The Church's vision is prophetic vision; it is always widening the view."

Because people perish where there is no vision. The prophetic passages of the Bible, given to remedy that lack, are accompanied almost invariably by words like these: "the *vision* of Isaiah," "the *word* of the Lord, which Isaiah *saw,*" "the Lord God *showed* Amos, and behold," "the *burden* of God which Habakkuk saw." Daniel saw *"visions* in his head as he lay on his bed"* and was told to "write the *dream* down." "The *word* of the Lord" was revealed to Jeremiah and a long list of other prophets. Flashes of revelation formed the messages of these prophets.

Though the writer of Hebrews reminded us that "in many and various ways God spoke to our fathers by the prophets," the oracle, or burden, was always mediated to the prophet by means of words or visions: what he heard, what he saw, or both were received from God for communication to a specified audience.

Why was an intermediary, such as a prophet, needed? (And why in our generation are artists sometimes given the role of seers?) Why wasn't the word transmitted directly, in its full blaze of light and meaning, to the entire human congregation? One of the symptoms of our human degeneracy is spiritual blindness. The disease of sin has damaged our souls' sensory receptors, and the "god of this world" makes it his priority to block or distort our view of God. Jehovah, by contrast, has become known to us as the revealer of hidden things or mysteries to his inner circle, especially through the prophets, and most of all through the Christ. It was Jesus who said, "To you it has been given to know the secrets of the kingdom of heaven" (Matthew 13:11 RSV).

The Almighty, in his intimate immanence and inscrutable otherness, who dwells in swift light and thick darkness, who administers tender love and implacable wrath, is mirrored in the profundities of philosophy and science, the fathomless ocean of ideas and words wrapped in mystery, the patterns of order observable in the deep forest, the wide wasteland. God is the Lord of creation. He is infinite, but in the finite creation, we may spy out his footprints.

In our own experiential wilderness, we are making trails, "clearing a way into being," as Heidegger suggested, without removing all the jutting rocks, the entangling vines, the rotting branches, which provide humus for the next generation of growth. No watertight system of theology or epistemology can exhaustively capture the realities of the universe, which must be "eaten," fragment by fragment. Unlike our Maker, we are finite; we cannot take in the world whole. But we may responsibly penetrate and revel in its every open aspect, remembering that while life is easy to annihilate, it is impossible to tame.

Reading O'Connor's letters in *The Habit of Being*, I often feel like heaving a sigh of relief. She somehow unites faith with a healthy skepticism. I can join her in saying:

> Faith is what you have in the absence of knowledge. . . . This clash doesn't bother me any longer because I have got, over the years, a sense of the immense sweep . . . of creation . . . of how incomprehensible God must necessarily be to be the God of heaven and earth. You can't fit the Almighty into your intellectual categories. . . . What kept me a skeptic in college was precisely my Christian faith: it always said, wait, don't bite on this, get a wider picture, continue to read.[8]

This is precisely where I am, and my thoughts link arms with O'Connor's words. I'm challenged when she admits, "It is much harder to believe than not to believe." But I want to shout, along with her, "You must at least do this: Keep an open mind. Keep it open toward faith, keep wanting it, keep asking for it, and leave the rest to God." Which is what I have been doing—wanting, asking, waiting . . .

Epiphany!—the showing of light—perhaps its very evanescence is what lends it its appeal. Most poets have epiphanies of sorts or they would not be writing, but in the poetic world today there seems to be little overarching sense of informing grace, yet the hunger in the darkness is there.

Three recurrent themes of contemporary poetry are incompleteness, impermanence, and incoherence—all true reflections of the human condition in its neurosis and fallenness. The despair of our times was vividly foreshadowed by William Butler Yeats:

> Turning and turning in the widening gyre
> The falcon cannot hear the falconer;
> Things fall apart; the centre cannot hold;
> Mere anarchy is loosed upon the world,
> The blood-dimmed tide is loosed, and everywhere
> The ceremony of innocence is drowned;
> The best lack all conviction, while the worst
> Are full of passionate intensity.[9]

Though many of the poems being written today contain poignant imagery borne along by words that are sharp as arrows, their essays at truth often miss the target. Of course, the challenge of *false* certainties is healthy. There are assumptions about God that *should* be shaken up. Transitions are always uncomfortable. There is generally a state of restlessness and disillusionment before spiritual renewal, and artists are often the first to sense this unsettledness.

But for true renewal, revival, a coming to life again, an awakening to meaning, the creative Spirit (capital *S*) must be freed in us. When this happens our lives are touched at every level. It is gnostic to think that only the "spiritual" part of us matters. If the Spirit is of God, he penetrates every aspect of our being and thinking, including the imagination.

And he will not be impeded or bound. When he moves, he is irresistible. "Where the Spirit of the Lord is, there is freedom" (2 Corinthians 3:17 NIV). Not disorder, not randomness, but a largeness that we, within our fragile walls of rules and regulations, may find threatening. None of our cultural conventions is safe from his encroachment—not even our systematic theologies, which are themselves artificial human inventions. Nor is the wilderness of the created world tidy any more than Aslan is tame.

But there is an order in death, decay, and renewal—there is a cycle in seeding, sprouting, leafing, flowering, fruiting, seeding, dying, rotting, and rebirth. At least for now, the death/decay part of the cycle is as necessary as the flower/fruit/seed. And poet Christians, if they are to reflect Creator and creation, must write the whole cycle into their work—the anguish as well as the celebration.

Think of the visions of Daniel. In the description of the "Being like the Son of Man," terrifying images appear—a face like lightning, blinding as the sun, eyes like blazing fire, arms and legs like bronze, glowing with furnace heat, a voice like a crashing waterfall, a message cutting as a double-edged sword. Daniel fell down at the sight, paralyzed with fear. He needed the reassurance of the words spoken to him, "Don't be afraid." And in that place he witnessed a revelation of both splendor and terror.

This last Sunday the homily was about Peter's affirmation of Christ as God. Part of me gladly makes that same affirmation. Another part of me hesitates and holds back. I thought of the cloud that covered Jesus and the disciples during the Transfiguration, a heavy fog that blocked Jesus from their sight. It seems that if we are disciples who want to be close to Jesus, as the three were, we must go through the darkness and unknowing of that cloud, or wait for it to lift and the Father to reveal the Son to us. Meanwhile, we live in the blinding mist on our way up the mountain.

An ice storm earlier this week caused the lights to go out all over town. Scanning the poems in *A Widening Light*, I chanced on Chad Walsh's poem, "Why hast though forsaken me?" and heard the words from Psalm 22 echoing my frequent feelings:

> *I have called to God and heard no answer,*
> *I have seen the thick curtain drop and sunlight die;*
> *My voice has echoed back, a foolish voice,*
> *The prayer restored intact*
> *To its silly source.*
> *I have walked in darkness, he hung in it.*
> *In all my mines of night he was there first;*
> *In whatever dead tunnel I am lost, he finds me.*
> *My God, my God, why hast thou forsaken me?*
> *From his perfect darkness a voice says, "I have not."*[10]

How can darkness be perfect? When it is part of God's purpose. Perhaps he planned this darkness, this power outage, as a demonstration, just as he planned it for his Son, so that the darkness may be banished when the power comes back. This way we see darkness for what it is—absence of light. It seemed a word of the Lord to me in the moment I read it. I can't see him—the darkness is too thick. All I want is a touch—hand, shoulder, robe—so that I know he is with me in this place until the lights come on and my eyes squint for the glory of it.

At church as we rehearsed fragments of the St. John Passion for two hours with orchestra and soloists. I didn't have a sense of the work as a whole. The basses were missing cues and earning the conductor's wrath. It's scary to think of a final performance when all feel so unready. But most of art and life and faith is like that.

Someone at chorale practice asked me if I was writing any poetry still, in the time of darkness after Harold's death. My answer: "Of course." Poetry is not detached. It grapples with issues of existence and reality and sorrow through a thousand lenses; the small happenings in which we search out ourselves and God refract the light into colored splinters. I have never lived so intensely or reflectively as I have recently, and writing is my best way to discover the meaning of it all. It is art translated from life. When I write poetry, I am translating my life into art.

In thinking, again, how the world seems to be divided into a dualism of light and dark, we see that in his humanity, Jesus was no stranger to darkness.

Though I am still sometimes nagged by darkness and doubts, whenever we pray the prayer of confession, I feel as if I am saying to God, *"Here I am, doubt running through me like a seam of coal in the rock. Take me as I am, Lord. I don't know how to be any different. Mine my coal, and kindle it. You alone can send the flame that will turn it into heat and light."*

Chapter Twelve

Tracing the Creative Process of Poets and Poems

WHAT MAKES A GREAT POET?

What makes for good poetry? The concentration of an idea or image to its essence, the crystallization in words of imagination and experience, the marriage of music and metaphor, economy—a paring away of the nonessential so that every word and phrase has weight and carries significance with the meaning of the whole being hinted at in the part; poems help us in our comprehension of the larger picture.

Perhaps we should first of all ask what we expect of a great poet, the person in whom poems begin. In *The Personal Heresy*, C. S. Lewis says, "The only two questions to ask about a poem, in the long run, are, firstly, whether it is interesting, enjoyable, attractive, and secondly, whether its enjoyment wears well and helps or hinders you towards all the other things you would like to enjoy, or do, or be."[1]

But there are other criteria. First, we are on the alert for the appearance and reappearance of themes that speak to the imagination and sensibilities of any age.

Second, we hope to see those primal themes tied down to earth with the concrete detail that exhibits an understanding of the daily concerns of common humanity, an understanding expressed in specific, visual, and sensuous images. (Lewis himself wrote earthy poetry. I am encouraged that his life was not limited to an ivory tower of the mind. He was asked by Mrs. Moore to scrub floors and help in making jam, tasks that kept him in touch with ordinary mortal life.)

Third, a great poet will continue over a lifetime to develop as an artist. With maturity should come depth, sureness, strength, insight, unself-conscious authority, and stylistic consistency without monotony.

Fourth, there must be significant growth in *quantity* as well as in *quality*. A great poet adds steadily to a body of work, growing to significant proportions over the years.

Fifth, a great poet must be, in some sense, a pioneer, working close to the cutting edge of innovation, attempting the original, the untried. She or he must constantly reinvent a personal style, not rut-bound; must attempt the experimental, the stylistic branching out. Even if it fails, it constitutes a form of growth.

Finally, in our list of the attributes of a great poet, there must be a magic at work, for, as Calvin Linton once said, "One cannot really explain *how* authentic poems work, for they work by magic, producing effects surpassing their visible means." A poem's unique magic is like human life—dissect the body and it is gone. It will not yield its essence to ruthless analysis.

What more is in poetry that makes it good? Surprise, surely. And delight. Words and lines that shine on the page. Encounters. Experience. Many dimensions—as opposed to a monochromatic or predictable presentation. A sense of music and rhythm. All these are elements that awaken an imaginative response in the reader.

The way to understand and enter a poet's work is not just by way of the mind, however, but by way of the heart and the imagination. A poem may fail to come to life even though it fulfills all the objective criteria for poetry. But if it moves us and illuminates us and wakes in us that peculiar pang of recognition that comes with vision, perhaps we can say that it succeeds.

That said, at the top of the list for good poetry stands the singing, surging imagination that stirs ideas into life so that they dart and hover in the mind long after the poem has been read.

I am a poet, not a scholar, and I admit to being a very subjective critic. And having said something about the writing of great poets, what more can I say about a poem—than that much of it *works for* me?

The genius of poetry is that it verbalizes what many people have felt without quite knowing how to express it. A poet brings the details into warm resonance on an emotional or spiritual level.

A poem begins often as a close-up of one small detail within a much larger picture. Imagine a landscape painting. You may take a magnifying glass and minutely examine the artist's brushwork in the lower right-hand corner of the canvas, where no direct image of the sky or distance appears and where there perhaps is only a faint gleam or shadow to indicate the existence of the sun elsewhere in the landscape. But the dark corner is just as true, artistically and spiritually, as the center of the painting with its brilliantly painted fields.

The poem is the little lens through which we can examine at close range the "insignificant" details of the universe, which then provide us with a miniature window on the world. In such small works of art the poet is lending the reader her eyes in hopes that those eyes will be captivated by things never noticed before—the true, dark corner perhaps.

It is helpful to remember that in literary poetry there is always some enigma; as Robert Frost observed, "A poem that is completely clear is a trifle glaring." What this means is that as poetry is read aloud, thoughtfully, allowing time and repeated readings to open up the layers of meaning within the writing, the reader's creative imagination must come alive and become almost as vital a part of the creative process as the artistic intent of the poet.

I am often asked, "How does a poem happen?" It's usually a rather mysterious event. Sometimes I'm asked to write an "occasional poem," designed specifically for a wedding or some other special event, but usually I find myself stirred by the sudden (and often inconvenient) arrival of an image or an idea or a resonant phrase that will not leave me alone. I may be thinking in the dark about the day's events and conversations just before going to sleep, or listening to NPR on my car radio, or setting up my tent at a campsite just before sunset, but this imperious idea will not be denied.

Sometimes this begins when I read another poet's evocative work. The spark of an image kindles my own imagination, and I am off, like a startled colt. At this point I am not quite responsible for my own actions. Preoccupied, I may forget an appointment or rush to my computer to type in this "breaking news" in fragmentary form. I suppose this is what makes a poet a poet—that slender antenna of awareness that is always extended, combing the air for images, listening to the rhythms of language, watching, noticing when something quite ordinary achieves an extraordinary significance that cries out to be crafted into an art form.

Poetry is both an art and a craft. The polishing of the poem on the page or the computer screen often takes dozens of rewrites over months or years. Poems I wrote twenty-five years ago, which have remained unfinished, wait like embryos in my file cabinet and may yet come alive for me as I find images and language that allow them to emerge from the birth canal and be born.

Where I live now, in the Pacific Northwest, my study window opens to a deep ravine guarded by cedars and banked with sword ferns, with a stream that sends its sounds into my thoughts and my writing. Sometimes I tell people, "I write best to the sound of running water." The shore of any ocean has much the same effect on me—its limitlessness, the borders of air and land and water chafing each other, the random treasures to be found and collected along the tide lines, many of which end up in poems. I catch myself saying—as I follow the edges of the incoming waves and pick up a pebble here, a shell there, an aqua winking eye of sea glass, a knot of driftwood, "This is the state of happiness. This is my purest happiness."

That old question raises its head: Why poetry, in a practical world? Because poetry enriches, it forces us to take time, slow down, reflect on what might otherwise escape our notice. It helps us to view life metaphorically instead of in terms of mere fact or information. Poetry helps us to become whole-brain people, teaching us to be thoughtful and creative in many areas of our lives. Most books that Christians read don't push them in this direction, where they can be quiet listeners. We're often pushed by the books we read toward busy-ness, efficiency, and self-ism. Poetry can help counter that. It opens up the windows to the whole universe, takes our eyes off ourselves, and often helps us to focus on Creator and creation.

The creative process begins, largely, in observation. But you also must be able to differentiate analyzing observations and feelings, then verbalizing them, then recording those words.

I crave an element of spontaneity and surprise in the creative process for a poem, not just using the obvious word but searching for the exact word or phrase that's right. You may settle on a word that startles you, but it's right.

In my own writing, I try to use the "nonpoetic" words of ordinary speech, rather than long polysyllabic strings of impenetrable or lofty language. I love the possibilities in everyday words and seek to bring them together in some form of juxtaposition that makes not only intellectual but poetic sense. The music of such lines rings in the ear. When that happens there's a sort of resonance in poetry—the words rub together to give off an almost electrical charge.

In a poem, many things work together—intelligence, music,

rhythm, imagination. This is not something that's easy to teach. A poet learns by practice in putting these elements together. Somehow we learn in the doing and by being our own best critics. The poem is wordplay. When it's going well, when I have waves of poems coming, I feel absolutely euphoric. It's a spontaneous, unpredictable joy, something that *takes me.*

I can't remember a time in my life when I *wasn't* writing poetry. I started as a very little girl, and it was my impression that this was a natural part of being human. Of course I didn't articulate it like that; I just thought that everybody wrote poetry. I suppose I started to write when I was five or six. Inspiration? I would just see pictures in my head and want to write about them.

I don't know where it came from, because though my father was a writer, he wrote only prose, in sermons and theological books. There were some artists among my aunts and uncles—but there was really nothing to encourage me except the fact that my dad carried around in his briefcase an anthology of modern English poets, and I knew that he loved them.

My own early writing was quite melodramatic. Obviously, it was not very good—this sort of thing: "I saw a loon against the moon / and knew of judgment following soon. / What was that? 'twas a footstep at the door, / nothing more." It rhymed and scanned and got me off to a running start.

By high school I began to win the annual poetry prize, and my poems would get printed in the yearbook. Then I went to college and declared an English major and a New Testament Greek minor. Clyde Kilby, a professor from whom I took every course he offered, gave me the encouragement and the impetus to do something with my poetry. He was open-minded enough to assign essays and papers to a whole class, while allowing me to work through the assignment in poetry form. On my paper, perhaps an epic poem, he'd write something like "Send this off to the *Atlantic* at once." With that kind of encouragement, I began to think seriously about poetry.

Since then there's been a gradual growth in terms of my acceptance and recognition as a poet. It's been a long, slow apprenticeship. And I still have much to learn. But I am grateful that my poetry now has a level of acceptance, both in Christian circles and in the general market.

In my writing life, one of the milestones was in the early '70s, when we were having a number of problems with our oldest adolescent child. We also had financial struggles, so we were crying out to God for help on every front—except for my poetry. I didn't want God to meddle with it. I feared that he would require me to make the poetry more holy, pious, or devotional and less earthy, less me. How myopic of me! I have learned since that God is larger than any poetry that I could write; his freedom and his wildness far exceed any human innovations.

God was always ready to come in—what was needed was a decision on my part to let go and follow the internal leading of my heart. I think the process of writing went on much as it had, but I became aware that I wasn't alone in it.

I think every poet, or any artist, has a sense of the muse. There's a waiting for the images and the ideas to be presented and then an alertness to catch them, and when they come, to record them. It's an unpredictable thing, difficult to anticipate.

Sometimes, like a baby being born, a poem will arrive in the middle of the night. And I have to pay attention at that moment; I can't just say, "Later, later." Because it's so central—there's a sense that *this is what my life is really all about*—that other activities become more peripheral, less imperative.

Most poets have the fear or panic that they've written their last poem and no more poems will ever be born. I've been through many a dry period and have gone months and months without a poem. I think I've learned not to worry about it anymore, because I know that it always comes back. Perhaps that's a little bit like the spiritual life; there are ups and downs and dry periods in which we learn things we couldn't learn in the more fruitful, fulfilling times of our lives.

My artistic work speaks out of the reality of personal experience. That's where its authenticity shows. If a reader can feel what the poet is feeling, what the poet is offering of an event or insight or emotion, then the transfer is complete. The gap has been bridged.

While my growth as a poet has its history, so does the development of each poem. Some poems begin as I'm reading in another field, science, for example, and an idea begs to be developed—thought through creatively.

Jules Verne was possibly the first speculative fiction writer of our contemporary age, writing his novel *The Desert of Ice* in the 1870s.

In the 1970s, the *Scientific American* took note of a device employed by Verne to extract his protagonists, a band of Arctic explorers, from a seemingly inextricable dilemma. Their wooden sailing ship had been crushed to splinters in the grip of polar ice,

leaving them stranded in the uninhabited and inhospitable
reaches of the polar ice cap. To rescue them and to provide his
novel with a more felicitous ending, Verne described how these
inventive adventurers carved a lens from clear ice, through which
they focused the sun's rays on wooden splinters from their ship,
kindling a lifesaving fire that allowed them heat enough to survive
until they were rescued. Implausible? *The Scientific American* edi-
tors thought so until they managed to duplicate the experiment
and kindle a flame using a lens of ice.

When I read the account of this paradoxical kindling of fire
from ice, my imagination was also kindled; the story called to me
to be written into a poem. Consider the resulting work, "Saved by
Optics":

> *First, they must find a chip of cold*
>
> *that has always wanted to see,*
> *to channel the light.*
> *Then, with hands devoid*
> *   of electricity*
>
> *without matches, even, and with only splinters*
> *of strength left*
>
> *they must carve it out—the rough*
> *eyeball—from under the brow of this ice continent*
>
> *and polish it between*
> *their curved palms' last warmth*
> *into the double convex*

of a lens
a gem without frost, or crack, cleansed by the flow
of its own tears.

Next, they must wait, shivering, for the slow sun
to reach the zenith
of his readiness

to work with them. Now. Focused in the eye
of ice

(angled exactly,
though its chill finds each
of their fingers' bones)

a matchless flame collects
until the concentrated scrutiny of light

reads the dry tinder into
a saving kindling—ice's gift
of heat, and paradox.[2]

I had felt no compelling theological motivation to write this poem, simply a fascination with an intriguing physical phenomenon. But much later, as I reread the completed poem with a more critical eye (the fires of composition having cooled), I became aware of some correspondences that had until then escaped my attention. Here was a group of helpless, hopeless human beings in a crisis of existential need, on the verge of extinction in the Arctic freeze, condemned to die by their own inability to create

enough warmth to survive. Cold *is* the antithesis of energy and
life, and they were utterly vulnerable to it, their own small internal wicks of flame too easily snuffed, their one source of heat
being the remote sun, its energy untapped until a creative mind
applied a simple principle of physics to the situation.

The link between the helpless humans ("without strength" from
Psalms 88:4 [NIV] is the biblical phrase that comes to mind) and
God—the source of all light, warmth, life—was a lens, and sponta-
neously I made the mental connection with Christ become human,
carved as it were from the ice continent itself, because he had "always
wanted" to be a channel for light. Once again the Incarnation is
there to be recognized as the central theological truth for our lives.

Further connections began to show up in my mind. This flaw-
less Christ, "a lens . . . without frost, or crack," his flame "matchless" (the wordplay also touches on the plight of having run out
of matches in the wilderness), was also fully human, weeping for
us and with us. Images of cold and heat, light and seeing, pervade
the poem, as does the idea of salvation and grace, appearing in
the "gift" of warmth.

"Now"—the moment of truth and transformation when the
sun's light becomes a searing pinpoint of heat—reminds us of the
verse in 2 Corinthians 6:2, "Now is the accepted time . . . the day
of salvation (NKJV)" to be patiently awaited throughout history. In
this context, the meaning that emerged for me was that the divine
and human Jesus Christ, God's lens, in whom divine love is
uniquely focused, translates the splintered, fragmented tinder of
our lives into something of life—enhancing value that can perpet-
uate the flame, just as the crystalline properties of the ice lens
turned the very cause of extinction—cold—into something of
life-giving value for Verne's heroes.

Another poem altogether, this one had a different coming-into-its-own history:

We Know This to Start With:

If we understood everything we wouldn't
be baffled. But mystery lives; somehow
without witchcraft or chicanery

we collect sounds and colors in a skyward
dish, like fruit in a bowl, and channel them
into verisimilitude—faces talking at us

from the tube's glass eye. Hallways of fog
enfold us in enigma. And then, the marvel of
window glass—how can anything be

hard enough to stop the hand and
hold its smudge while letting through this
soft light? The one wheat kernel that

breeds a thousand—a miracle of
loaves over and over again.
The stars, invisible in the blind day,

revealed, thick as pollen, by the absence
of light. A billion spiky grass blades that melt
into a perfectly flat horizon. The Holy Ghost

waking me in my bedroom, drenching my
dry heart with fluid syllables, breathing
flesh onto the fetal bones of this poem. [3]

I began to write this poem on a plane as it was taxiing out to
the runway in Kalispell, Montana. I had just spent a week of
retreat by a lake with several women friends. It had been a time of
listening for God's voice as my mind and body achieved stillness
and settled in to the peace of my security in Christ after a compli-
cated year of frenzied activity on several different fronts.

During that week I had indeed met God, or at least I had had a
powerful glimpse of him, and I wanted to hold on to the imprint of
the holy on my soul as I had experienced it in that vast and beautiful Montana landscape. But I have learned that the harder you try
to grasp at transcendent experience, the quicker it evaporates. And
for me this signifies what the life of faith is about—believing, holding on to truth even though the epiphany has vanished and my
understanding of it was limited in the first place.

As the plane dawdled along the runway, I noticed a satellite dish
angled at the sky, catching its signals out of the atmosphere, like
butterflies in a net, and the words and phrases began to form in my
mind. The poem took off as the plane took off: "We know this to
start with: / If we understood everything we wouldn't / be baffled.
But mystery lives—"

Then my imagination began to pull in some of the enigmas of
our daily human lives, with me jotting them into my journal—
how television works to capture and carry images around the
world, how one seed can breed a thousand, the flattening effect of
distance, and particularly the mystery of how a poem comes into
being as my imagination is quickened. At home, later that night,

other lines and images wakened me, and by daybreak the first draft of the poem had completed itself.

The process always has notes of the unanticipated and the unpredictable. Over the years, my writing has gradually changed from being more abstract to being more concrete, poem by poem. You learn from your own creative process, from trying out various techniques and styles and ways of coming at a story or poem. My computer is full of seeds of ideas and uncompleted poems that haven't found themselves yet. There's a lot of trial and error; I'm never sure when a thing is going to succeed. And when is a piece finished? You may find yourself continuing to revise until the writing seems to settle into itself and feel complete. Yet you still invite the ideas and follow them where they go, developing them through craft.

It's like a child growing in spurts—so unpredictable, you don't know what the final result will be. Does that make it sound as though the artist has no control at all? That's not true. The artist indeed supervises and records the growth of a piece of writing, but there's a balance between having control and letting go, letting the writing find its own destiny, its own way. You must let it develop itself—which is like raising a child. In the early stages, the parents are very much in control of the young life, but as the child grows older and learns how to make choices and decisions, that child begins to take destiny in his own hands and shape his own life in different ways.

While we don't often know what the final product will be, many of you have had, I am sure, the experience of working on a speech or a course or writing a paper and of being joyfully astonished as a serendipitous idea flies into your mind or appears on the pages of the very magazine you are reading, or the information that comes in casual conversation proves to be the precise link needed to complete your chain of thought.

In both faith and art, we sense the significance of the ordinary, of seemingly trivial events and circumstances—the "harsh particulars" of polar ice and lovemaking and weeds and wet weather and age-spots and agates in the surf.

Both faith and art exist because things contain and mediate meaning; it seems impossible to name anything that is simply random or incidental. As we experience the cause and effect of answers to prayer, a pattern becomes observable. We sometimes sense that the Power that orders the universe is ordering our lives, causing an ordinary day to explode with meaning. This is where the serendipity effect appears. (In writing a poem in which I describe the flight of a gull, I wanted to use the phrase describing the bird's "up-thrusting eye." My keyboard knew better, and without my realizing it, substituted "up-trusting," which fulfilled the metaphor far more powerfully.)

This is the inexplicable nature of art. Robert Olen Butler observed that as ideas grow and take form and you as an artist engage with it, "you thrum to a work of art. You don't understand it intellectually."

Appendix A

Writing Exercises and Questions for Discussion

PART I

CHAPTER 1: THE CREATIVE HEART OF GOD

1. Has a friend or relative ever asked you, "What good is art?" Have you wondered how to respond? In your journal or in a letter addressed to this friend or relative, respond to this question (you don't have to send this letter unless you'd like to). You may even wish to develop this letter into an artist's statement.

2. Have you found yourself looking at the small lights of the night sky in wonder? Have you looked at the ocean and found joy at the motion and color of waves? Has this ever moved you to try to describe this beauty? Or to interpret it in an art form? With

a group or in your journal, explore how God's creation forms our understanding of beauty.

3. The Old Testament book of Genesis and the New Testament gospel of John focus on the importance of the creative act of words—the Word. When God breathed a word in the first chapter of Genesis, his word suddenly became a created *thing*. As an artist, a writer, how does knowing this breathing Word—the Logos, Jesus—inform the way you look at creativity?

CHAPTER 2: ENTERING INTO BEAUTY

1. Think of examples of times you encountered beauty. What beautiful object, literature, experience, or landscape moves and exhilarates you? How would you define beauty? How important is it in your life?

2. In the light of church history, why do you think the contemporary Christian church has suspected, despised, or ignored art and artists to such an extent? Do you sense any change happening in church communities today?

3. What factors in the frenetic action-orientation of our society mitigate against the appreciation and pursuit of art and beauty?

4. How can we, as Christians, as artists, begin to restore beauty, the creative imagination, and art to their rightful place in the life and worship of the church?

CHAPTER 3: MEETING THE GOD OF METAPHOR

1. Start with word association. Pick one metaphor word that seems to have significance for you, that fits your personality, gifts, inclinations, and circumstances, such as, *springtime, rain, baby, shadow, seed, green, shell, pebble, ship, unfolding flower, river, rock*. You may wish to use an image from the Bible, such

as a *lamp, branch, vine, deer, temple, water channel, sheep, pilgrim, pearl, farmer, athlete, field*. For a few moments, allow this word or image to plant a picture in your mind. Allow your senses and your imagination to enlarge on this image. What do you feel, taste, smell, hear, or otherwise notice about it?

2. For several minutes jot down all the words and ideas that this word brings to mind, clustering them around it as the nucleus for brainstorming a web of word bubbles, all with lines attached to the circle around the main word.

3. Over the next few days, tie the most potent of these associated ideas together by building a personal psalm, a poem, an essay, a meditation, or a story around this central metaphor, which is you. Keep it personal and concrete (not abstract or general-ized), and use everyday (not religious or "poetic") language.

   When this has taken shape, ask yourself: If I live out this metaphor fully, what might be the results in my personal/ spiritual growth? In my attitude toward my Creator? In the lives and relationships of those around me? In my community of writers? In the world I live in? Use these questions as the basis for an essay about yourself and your personal metaphor.

4. If this is a time of decision or transition in your life, ask God to show you a personal metaphor that will inform you as you meditate, praying for wisdom and guidance.

   Imagine yourself, for instance, as clay being shaped into some useful or beautiful ceramic piece. As you spin on the potter's wheel, you may feel dizzy and weak. But remember, the Potter's strong hands are holding you centered, shaping you into just what he has in mind for you—some useful and beautiful object or container for his house. And when he is through molding you, you may even have to go through the kiln of struggle. But the fired pottery is worth all the steps in the process.

Chapter 4: Learning from Story

1. *Story* is the way Jesus explored spiritual truths and asked spiritual questions. How might you—as a poet, writer, painter, dancer, actor—explore a story in your life in order to frame questions that relate spiritual truth?

2. How is it that stories and parables continue working on us at deeper levels, long after the story has been told?

3. *"The story of the world is imprinted everywhere—the growth rings widening in the boles of trees, the wind- and water-carved art of coastal sandstone rocks, sharp 'young' mountains like the Tetons."*

    Revisit some imprinted story, look to a landscape or seascape, or even watch an aging neighbor's slow walk to the grocery store, down a city block. As you imaginatively trace their stories, watch the world unfold in a new way. If you are a visual artist, incorporate this in some way into your work.

4. Think back on this Eugene Peterson phrase: *"Story isn't imposed on our lives; it invites us into its life."*[1] Explore a time when you have been invited into the life of story. How did that change you, inform you? How might that change the way you view the creative process?

5. If story is the *"the most familiar and accessible way for human beings to understand the world,"* think of the ways you have understood or explored the world through story.

Chapter 5: Celebrating Imagination

1. If you remember a time early in your creative life that you discovered a "widening of the imagination," explore this developmental stage in your writing.

Writing Exercises and Questions for Discussion   191

2. What does a "baptized imagination" look like? Consider reading a story from the Old Testament or a parable from the gospel texts, or the vivid imagery of Revelation. Ask yourself, What does the baptized imagination look like in this text? Can I read between the lines, imaginatively? Or, How does this Scripture help form a baptized imagination in me?

3. Perhaps you grew up in a family or faith culture that did not encourage *imagination*. If so, where did you first meet and recognize the power of imagination? How is imagination God's gift for expressing spiritual truths?

4. Take a portion of a psalm or a gospel text for meditation. How would you see this differently if you brought your heart, mind (including the imagination), and soul to engage with the text? Discover how using your own name, or personal pronouns, refreshes and personalizes your understanding of the text.

   If bringing imagination to prayer and meditation is intimidating, reread Chapter 4. As you read, keep your psalm or chosen Scripture text alongside for reference. Then prayerfully—and perhaps playfully—bring your imagination into this place before God as God brings imagination and play into the text of Scripture for you.

Chapter 6: Listening to the Muse

1. If you keep a journal, look through pages of previous years for a passage that leaps out—such as this *knitting* and *being knit* section. Look for pages that point to spiritual understanding coming through a creative act. If you don't keep a journal, think back to a time where a simple or creative act—painting, doing photography, washing a car, planting an herb garden—sud-

denly informed all of your senses, teaching you anew about creativity or faith.

2. We are often afraid of silence, of being alone. Yet we know from the mystics and the contemplatives that this silence before God is often meaningful, rich, and creative. It may also be challenging and raw. What are ways that we might develop an open silence before God, a listening silence? What are possible barriers in our lives to this creative silence?

3. Read again the short section from which this quote is taken: *"Spirituality is very like the creative impulse toward art—often fickle and unpredictable. We have an untamable, undomesticated Spirit."*

   Have you ever wanted to tame or to domesticate the Holy Spirit? Tame your art? Why do we often desire to bring the Holy Spirit and art into the realm of understanding and quantifying? What spiritual disciplines or tools might you explore that could help you keep hands and hearts open to the guidance of the Holy Spirit, wherever that may lead you?

4. Like Denise Levertov, have you ever experienced the process of writing a poem or creating a piece of art that brought about your transformation—even a conversion? What are the places in your art and in your life that you have been changed by the work itself?

PART II
CHAPTER 7: BEGINNING WITH JOURNAL WRITING

1. Consider keeping a daily reflective journal for images, ideas, wonderments, questions. If a commitment to journal keeping over a long stretch of time sounds daunting, give yourself only

a week or a month to explore this new form. Start with simple questions like these: What made me glad, today? Or sad? Or mad? Or afraid?

2. If you already keep a journal, how have you discovered that writing through emotional issues or pain has allowed you to see these hurts in a new way?

3. Henri Nouwen wrote about the necessity of writing to explore our deepest interior places: "I do not yet know what I carry in my heart, but I trust that it will emerge as I write."[2]

   If there is some question you have been pondering, some joy you have wanted to explore more fully through writing, give voice to that question or joy. Write about it in the open spaces of your journal paper. Observe what emerges from your heart. Note any surprising conclusions.

4. If you don't know how to begin keeping a journal but you'd like to try, you might start out by "reading, reading, reading" until a line of a poem or a word from a psalm speaks out in a profound way.

   Capture that line by copying it into your journal, then respond to it with your own thoughts by describing how that line affected you, or how that image reminded you of a forgotten memory.

Chapter 8: Learning to Risk

1. Write in your journal about a time when you took a great risk in "charting a course"—a risk that challenged you to your core—yet in which you discovered something amazing about yourself or God in the process. Write about this experience and what it taught you about risk, about creativity, about faith.

2. If you *want* to move toward risk in your creativity but don't know where to begin, write openly about the possible sources for your hesitancy. You might also want to brainstorm for creative approaches to risk, which help you say yes to new ideas, a new path.

3. List three "risk-taking" goals in faith and in creative life that you'd like to explore. The list may be as simple as listening to a new kind of music. Or taking an art class. Or, if you're a visual artist, maybe the risk would be to take a writing course.

    Think imaginatively about your three risks, and develop a course of action to begin each one.

4. Do you find yourself always "coloring inside the lines"? Look at the life of Jesus in the Gospels. Find one or two stories in the life of Jesus that contain examples of coloring outside the lines. How might you be challenged to look anew at your own life of faith, your own creative life, in light of these stories?

CHAPTER 9: PAYING ATTENTION

1. If you are writing in a group, free-write for about fifteen minutes about something "small but significant" about yourself. Regather and share what you have learned with the larger group.

    Remember: *We must learn to be still; we can't see our true reflections in running water.*

2. Write a letter to God telling him that you are deliberately setting aside the large and heavy responsibilities that dominate your everyday life in order to listen to God and his "still, small voice." (List your "life baggage," your burdens, and then give them to God to care for, for the remainder of the week.) As you listen, can you hear God saying anything to you? Write it down.

CHAPTER 10: CULTIVATING CREATIVITY

1. What does your creative process look like? Where do your "seed ideas" come from? And how do you transform these seed ideas into larger creative art forms?

2. How do you develop your skills and craft? If you're a painter, do you work alongside of other painters? If you work as a photographer, what disciplines help shore up your composition? Your darkroom skills?

   This coming month challenge yourself with three goals for your art milestones that will help you move to the next level of fluency or skill.

3. *"For the Christian artist there will always be some attempt, also in nonverbal art forms (such as sculpture, dance, mime, or instrumental music), to reduce anarchy to order; to reflect reality and moral/spiritual values, however indirectly; to contrast light with darkness, discord with harmony; to achieve a kind of balance."*

   In your art, what are the ways you move toward order and reflect reality? Does this come naturally, as the result of a life lived in faith? Or do you intentionally develop this in your art?

4. Do you have a group from your church, or a local arts group that supports your creative work? If so, list the ways in which this group is collaborative and assists you in avenues of art. Bring that list of gifts of support to God, thanking him for the abundance.

   If you are not part of an arts group, consider forming one. No need to start large. One or two people may begin meeting in a coffee shop, joining in conversations about artistic challenges and creative ideas.

5. If your church group is supportive, consider organizing an arts day at your church, for local artists to show their work; or con-

sider finding a sponsor for a coffeehouse, where poems can be read or musicians invited to participate.

Chapter 11: Understanding the Shadow Side of Creativity

1. There are many of us who struggle with the question, Is God capricious? And that question mark may continue through our lives. If you keep a journal, write about an experience of the hiddenness of God. Looking back, what discoveries did you make during that dark time?

2. If you are a visual artist, explore through painting or photography how *chiaroscuro* works. Explore how light reveals the darkness, how darkness reveals light.

3. C. S. Lewis wrote, "best havings are wantings." This is an unusual way to see our desires. Indeed, we often find ourselves disappointed when desires are left unfulfilled.

    What areas of your life speak to the *best havings* being seen as *wantings?*

4. For artists, delving into mystery and fathomlessness sometimes opens into epiphany—as with the Eucharist. Where have you met this mystery and epiphany lately?

Chapter 12: Tracing the Creative Process of Poets and Poems

1. Even if your form of creativity is not poetry, there are ways of listening to the multitude of language and sounds. These bring awareness to any form of creativity. Visit a place of noise and bustle or even of great silence, and journal about an unusual sound that you hear for the first time—or some old sound or a way of silence that affects you anew.

2. *"A great poet adds steadily to a body of work growing to significant proportions over the years."*

    If you are a poet or a fiction writer or a visual artist, give yourself the chance to tour your work over the years. Trace in your journal the ebbs and flows, the growth spurts, the joys, the detours, the change of directions. As you observe these places of growth and change, write in your journal about the changes in your work, perhaps analyzing how it has become more complex or more mature.

3. *"Encounters.—Experiences. Observations. Impulses. Emotions. Exuberance. A sense of rhythm or music. Resonant phrases. Surprises. Impressions. Significant details.*

    This list describes some characteristics of a good poem. Yet this might also suggest standards of excellence in other art forms. In reading a poem or looking at a painting or listening to a sonata, have you ever met the joining of all these characteristics? Write about how you recognized this combination of characteristics as a profound gathering of riches or how you sensed you were in the presence of greatness.

Creativity Books—A Reading List

I. Prose Writers and Books on Creativity

These books are all good introductions to the creative process or the formation and nurturing of creativity. All provide a way to begin, to see the creative process as an essential value.

David Bayles and Ted Orland, *Art and Fear*
Walter Brueggemann, *Finally Comes the Poet,* and *The Prophetic Imagination*
Annie Dillard, *Holy the Firm* and *The Writing Life*
Janice Elsheimer, *The Creative Call*
Brewster Ghiselin, ed., *The Creative Process*
Natalie Goldberg, *Writing Down the Bones*
Anne Lamott, *Bird by Bird*
Madeleine L'Engle, *Walking on Water*
Denise Levertov, *Light Up the Cave* and *New and Selected Essays*
Gerald May, *The Wisdom of Wilderness*
Rollo May, *The Courage to Create*
Leyland Ryken, *The Christian Imagination*

Dorothy Sayers, *The Mind of the Maker*
Francis Schaeffer, *Art and the Bible*
Gene Edward Veith, *The Gift of Art*

II. POETS AND POETRY BOOKS

I encourage you to begin with the classical poets, particularly the meta-physical poets, such as John Donne and George Herbert. Read Shakespeare aloud. Or Milton. Anthologies bring together poetry of a certain period or with a common theme. Check out books from the library, or buy books of contemporary poetry at general bookstores. Read the poems aloud more than once. Let the sound of the words sink into your mind.

Wendell Berry, *A Timbered Choir*
Emily Dickinson, *Collected Poems*
Robert Frost, *Collected Poems*
Jeanine Hathaway, *The Self as Constellation*
Seamus Heaney, *The Spirit Level*
George Herbert, *Collected Poems*
Gerard Manley Hopkins, *Poems*
Andrew Hudgins, *Saints and Strangers* and *Babylon in a Jar*
Mark Jarman, *The Green Man, Questions for Ecclesiastes,* and *Unholy Sonnets*
Jane Kenyon, *Let Evening Come* and *Otherwise*
Galway Kinnell, *Imperfect Thirst*
Madeleine L'Engle *The Weather of the Heart* and *The Ordering of Love*
Paul Mariani *Deaths and Transfigurations*
Sharon Olds, *The Father*
Mary Oliver, *Why I Wake Early* and *Thirst*
Linda Pastan, *Heroes in Disguise.*
Rainer Maria Rilke, *Letters to a Young Poet*
Rumi, *The Soul of Rumi* (translated by Coleman Barks)
Gjertrud Schnackenberg, *The Lamplit Answer*
R. S. Thomas, *Counterpoint*
Jeanne Murray Walker, *A Deed to the Light*
Richard Wilbur, *Mayflies* and *The Things of This World*

Acknowledgments

$\mathcal{I}$t would be almost impossible for me to mention all the ways I have received help along the way, over many years, in developing the ideas in this book, which has come together in company with countless kindred spirits whose insights have sharpened my own. I have been privileged to have as friends writers and artists whose reputations and resumes far exceed my own. But here's an attempt to name some sources of help:

Students in courses I have taught at Regent College, who often helped me to say, in response to challenges and questions, what I didn't know I knew. Participants in many retreats and conferences in North America and overseas whose creative thinking enlarged my own.

My colleagues in the Chrysostom Society whose challenges to my thinking and whose friendship and collegiality have multiply blessed my life for the past twenty-one years.

Karen Cooper, close friend and scholar, whose own writing and research often clarified mine, whose detailed readings of my poetry often helped make it what it is, and who always gave me her unqualified support when I was struggling.

Jeanne Murray Walker, whose generous life and writing often kept me afloat and with whom I have shared adventures overseas and flotillas of new poems.

John Shaw, my son, a clear-eyed critic and imaginative thinker who was often able to draw out from my confusion what I really wanted to say. Starbucks and good coffee contributed to this process over months and years.

To others, part of the continuum of my life, I owe deep thanks —Greg Wolfe, Patti Pierce, Barbara Braver, Jennifer Bullis, Lydia McCauley, Fr. Kevin Allen, Fr. David Denney, and especially my husband, John Hoyte.

David Thornton, who under the pressure of blizzards and heavy family responsibilities, scanned and retyped for this book many yellowed typescripts from my files, often working late into the night to meet my deadlines.

My agent, Lee Hough, whose help and support is always meaningful.

Finally, Lil Copan, to whom I owe an enormous debt of gratitude for her gift—many weeks of her own time unraveling into a coherent whole the tangled mess of essays, lectures, poems, and journal notes that I had thrust upon her. With skill and efficiency she sorted and re-ordered materials of mine in a task that had seemed impossible to me, too close as I was to my own writing.

Notes

Introduction

1. C.S. Lewis, *The Weight of Glory* (San Francisco: HarperCollins, 1980), 140. © C. S. Lewis Pte. Ltd. Reprinted by permission.
2. Jeanne Murray Walker, *Nailing Up the Home Sweet Home* (Cleveland: Cleveland State University Poetry Center, 1980).
3. Czeslaw Milosz, Nobel Peace Prize Acceptance Speech, 1980, © The Nobel Foundation.
4. John Fowles quoted in "Mysterious Movers and Shakers a Maggot," by Christopher Porterfield, *Time*, 9 September 1985.

Chapter 1

1. Alexsandr Solzhenitzyn, Nobel Peace Prize Acceptance Speech, 1970, © The Nobel Foundation.
2. Thomas A. Kempis, *Imitation of Christ* (Peabody, MA: Hendrickson, 2004).
3. Luci Shaw, *Polishing the Petoskey Stone* (Vancouver: Regent College Publishing, 2003), 3.
4. Arthur Koestler, *The Sleepwalkers: A History of Man's Changing Vision of the Universe* (New York: Random, 1959, 1990).
5. Robert Farrar Capon, *The Third Peacock: The Problem of Good and Evil* (Minneapolis: Winston Press, 1986).
6. "Christmas, Whidbey Island," by Loren Wilkinson. Used by permission.

Chapter 2

1. Francis Schaeffer, *Art and the Bible* (Downers Grove, IL: Intervarsity, 1973).
2. John Walford, *Art and the Christian Today* (Grantham, PA: Messiah College, 1985).
3. Luci Shaw, *Polishing the Petoskey Stone* (Vancouver: Regent College Publishing, 2003), 33.
4. Eugene Peterson, *Leap Over a Wall* (New York: HarperCollins, 1997), 86.

Chapter 3

1. William Barclay, *The Mind of Jesus* (New York: Hyperion, 1990).
2. C.S. Lewis, *A Grief Observed* (New York: HarperCollins, 2001) © C. S. Lewis Pte. Ltd. Reprinted by permission.
3. C.S. Lewis, *The Weight of Glory* (San Francisco: HarperCollins, 1980) © C. S. Lewis Pte. Ltd. Reprinted by permission.
4. William Stafford, *The Way It Is* (St. Paul, MN: Graywolf Press, 1999).
5. Thomas Howard, *Chance or The Dance* (Ft. Collins, CO: Ignatius Press, 1989).Used by permission.

6. Virginia Stem Owens, "Black and White and Read All Over," *Christianity Today*.

7. Robert Farrar Capon, *The Third Peacock: The Problem of Good and Evil* (Minneapolis: Winston Press, 1986).

8. John Stott, *God's Book for God's People* (Downers Grove, IL: Intervarsity, 1982).

9. Luci Shaw, *Polishing the Petoskey Stone* (Vancouver: Regent College Publishing, 2003), 49.

10. C.S. Lewis, *The Pilgrim's Regress* (Grand Rapids: Wm. Eerdmans, 1992) © C. S. Lewis Pte. Ltd. Reprinted by permission.

11. Luci Shaw, *The Sighting* (Colorado Springs: Harold Shaw, division of WaterBrook, 1981), 95.

Chapter 4
1. Eugene Peterson, *Leap Over a Wall* (New York: HarperCollins, 1997), 3–4.

2. Brewster Ghiselin, *The Creative Process: Reflections on Invention in the Arts and Sciences* (Berkeley, CA: University of California Press, 1985), 174.

Chapter 5
1. James Brabazon, *Dorothy L. Sayer: A Biography* (New York: Avon, a division of HarperCollins, 1982).

2. Ibid.

3. C.S. Lewis, *George MacDonald, An Anthology* (Carmichael, CA: Touchstone Books, 1996) © C. S. Lewis Pte. Ltd. Reprinted by permission.

Chapter 6
1. C.S. Lewis, *Mere Christianity* (New York: Scribner, 1997), 120. © C. S. Lewis Pte. Ltd. Reprinted by permission.

2. Annie Dillard, *Teaching a Stone to Talk* (New York: HarperCollins, 1988).

3. Dorothy L. Sayers, *Gaudy Night* (New York: HarperCollins, 1936), 186.

4. C. S. Lewis, "It All Began with a Picture," in *On Stories and Other Essays on Literature* (New York: Harcourt, Brace, and Jovanovich, 1982), 53. © C. S. Lewis Pte. Ltd. Reprinted by permission.

5. Ibid.

6. Luci Shaw, *Writing the River* (Vancouver: Regent College Publishing, 2003), 36.

7. May Sarton, *Mrs. Stevens Hears the Mermaids Singing* (New York: W.W. Norton, 1993).

8. Denise Levertov, *New & Selected Essays* (New York: New Directions, 1992), 249.

9. Ibid., 250.

Chapter 7
1. Luci Shaw, *The Green Earth* (Grand Rapids: Wm. Eerdmans, 2002), 57.

2. Robert Durback,ed., *Seeds of Hope: A Henri Nouwen Reader* (New York: Bantam,1989), 28.

Chapter 8
1. Walter Bruggemann, *Finally Comes the Poet: Daring Speech for Proclamation* (Minneapolis: Fortress Press, 1989).
2. Madeleine L'Engle, *Walking on Water* (Colorado Springs: Harold Shaw, division of WaterBrook, 1980), 161.

Chapter 9
1. Luci Shaw, *Polishing the Petoskey Stone* (Vancouver: Regent College Publishing, 2003).
2. Sir Arthur Conan Doyle, *Sherlock Holmes: A Scandal in Bohemia.* ©1892.
3. Mary Oliver, *New and Selected Poems* (Boston: Beacon Press, 1993).
4. Annie Dillard, "The Meaning of Life," *Life Magazine,*
5. Annie Dillard, *Pilgrim at Tinker Creek* (New York: HarperCollins, 2007).
6. "Two Voices in a Meadow," from *The Poems of Richard Wilbur* (New York: Harcourt Brace, 1963), 5.
7. Gene Edward Veith, Jr., *The Gift of Art* (Downers Grove, IL: InterVarsity, 1983), 19.
8. Ibid., 43.

Chapter 10
1. Amy Lowell quoted in *The Creative Process* (Berkeley: University of California Press, 1985), 110 ff.
2. Ibid., 123.
3. Igor Stravinsky, *An Autobiography* (W. W. Norton & Company, 1998).
4. Luci Shaw, "Ice Box Poem." Used by permission.

Chapter 11
1. To read more about Gerald May and his writing visit www.shalem.org.
2. Ron Hansen, *Mariette in Ecstasy* (New York: HarperCollins, 1991).
3. C.S. Lewis, *Letters*, 5 November 1959. © C. S. Lewis Pte. Ltd. Reprinted by permission.
4. C.S. Lewis, *The Problem of Pain* (New York: HarperCollins, 2001) © C. S. Lewis Pte. Ltd. Reprinted by permission.
5. Luci Shaw, *God in the Dark* (Vancouver: Regent College Publishing, 1998).
6. William Johnston, ed., *The Cloud of Unknowing* (New York: Image, 1996).
7. "Evangelism Plus" *Christianity Today,* http://www.christianitytoday.com/ct/2006/october/32.94.html
8. Sally Fitzgerald, ed., *The Habit of Being: Letters of Flannery O'Connor* (New York: Farrar Straus and Giroux, 1999).
9. William B. Yeats, *Later Poems* (London: Macmillan, 1931).

10. Luci Shaw, ed., *A Widening Light* (Vancouver: Regent College Publishing, 1997).

Chapter 12
1. C.S. Lewis, *The Personal Heresy* (London: Oxford University Press, 1965) © C. S. Lewis Pte. Ltd. Reprinted by permission.
2. Luci Shaw, *Polishing the Petoskey Stone* (Vancouver: Regent College Publishing, 2003), 227.
3. Luci Shaw, *The Angles of Light* (Colorado Springs: Harold Shaw, a division of Waterbrook, 2000), 17.

Appendix A
1. Eugene Peterson, *Leap Over a Wall* (New York: HarperCollins, 1997), 3–4.
2. Luci Shaw, lectures notes from Christian Imagination class, 2/24/99.